Of Flowers & a Village

Of Flowers & a Village

by

WILFRID BLUNT

An Entertainment for Flower Lovers

Illustrated by
RICHARD SHIRLEY SMITH

With a Foreword by
JAMES J. WHITE

TIMBER PRESS

First published in 1963 by Hamish Hamilton, Ltd.
Foreword copyright © 2006 by Timber Press, Inc.

Published in 2006 by
Timber Press, Inc.
The Haseltine Building
133 S.W. Second Avenue, Suite 450
Portland, Oregon 97204-3527, U.S.A.
www.timberpress.com
For contact information regarding editorial, marketing, sales, and
distribution in the United Kingdom, see www.timberpress.co.uk.

Printed in China

Library of Congress Cataloging-in-Publication Data

Blunt, Wilfrid, 1901–
    Of flowers & a village : an entertainment for flower lovers / byWilfrid Blunt ;
illustrated by Richard Shirley Smith ; with a forewordby James J. White.
       p. cm.
    Originally published: London : Hamish Hamilton Ltd., 1963.
    Includes bibliographical references.
    ISBN-13: 978-0-88192-778-8
    ISBN-10: 0-88192-778-3
    1. Gardens. 2. Gardening. I. Title.
    SB455.B55 2006
    635.9—dc22

                                                        2005029465

A catalog record for this book is available from the British Library.

Foreword

WILFRID BLUNT was an accomplished man of arts and letters, and his influence continues today in many fields. I knew him best for his classic *The Art of Botanical Illustration*, but his other titles of botanical interest also include *Tulipomania; Great Flower Books* (with Sacheverell Sitwell); the *Hortulus* of Walahfrid Strabo (with Raef Payne and G. H. M. Lawrence); *The Compleat Naturalist: A Life of Linnaeus; In for a Penny, a Prospect of Kew Gardens: Their Flora, Fauna and Falballas;* and *The Illustrated Herbal* (with Sandra Raphael).

His subjects for books were by no means confined to plants but extended to interesting people of any period who struck his fancy—including a king, a composer, an artist, a museum director, and early travelers in the Middle East and Central Asia. His meticulously researched and engagingly written biographies included not only his subjects' good deeds but also their "faults and shortcomings . . . warts and all." Other of his diverse subjects included Japanese color prints, scripts and handwriting, the architecture and arts of Islam, and the London zoo. He wrote for the general reader but viewed his writings as a jumping-off point for those wishing to learn more.

i

Authors and editors regularly called upon him to contribute introductions, forewords, and chapters, and for eighteen months he was a garden columnist for the *Sunday Times*. He completed two volumes of autobiography, *Married to a Single Life* and *Slow on the Feather*. A third, to be titled *Over My Dead Body*, was to appear posthumously, but by 1986 he wrote that it would never be written—he no longer had the energy.

Blunt studied music and did some public singing in the 1930s. He was an art master at Haileybury College (1923–38) and drawing master at Eton College (1938–59). In 1959 he was appointed to the new post of curator of the Watts Gallery at Compton, near Guildford in Surrey. He announced this post-retirement position in a letter to George H. M. Lawrence, the first director of the Hunt Institute for Botanical Documentation at Carnegie Mellon University (then Carnegie Tech) in Pittsburgh, Pennsylvania—the earliest of many Blunt letters in the Hunt's archive.

Regarding *Of Flowers & a Village*, Blunt wrote to Lawrence in June 1962, "I finished, only this week, a rather frivolous book about flowers, which I fear may contain one or two things that will shock botanists & gardeners! I only hope they will accept it as a *jeu d'esprit*, and not be too serious about it." Four months later he wrote: "I'm still at work on this rather frivolous flower-book I think I mentioned to you; I *thought* I had finished it, but constantly find things to add & to alter. I only hope I shan't make *too* many enemies through it in the botanical world, & that readers will realize that it's *meant* to be mostly funny!" "Dewbury," the village in question, was closely based on Compton.

The residents were aware that Blunt was writing this book and shuddered to think what scandals he might reveal. When it was published, those who were unmentioned lamented their absence!

Imagine my joy in the late 1960s and early 1970s upon discovering, in a museum bookstore, Blunt's classic book on botanical art, as well as a miscellany of artworks filed alongside the dried specimens in the herbaria of the U.S. National Arboretum and the Smithsonian Institution's Museum of Natural History. This was well before the formation of the Guild of Natural Science Illustrators, the Society of Botanical Artists (U.K.), and the American Society of Botanical Artists, and before the travel exhibitions and books of the collection of Dr. Shirley Sherwood in England—all of which give credence to the fact that Blunt was a pioneer in popularizing the genre of botanical art.

A botanical artist himself, Blunt's 1948 watercolor of a snowdrop (*Galanthus nivalis*) was included in one of the Hunt Institute's international exhibitions (1988). His entry in that catalog was expedited, as I had for some time been compiling a Blunt bibliography (with the assistance of artist Jenny Brasier, who, in fact, lent the watercolor; then Hunt Institute librarian Bernadette Callery; and Mr. Blunt). My one visit with Blunt, on September 7, 1984, was due to the kindness of Brasier, whose artistic talent Blunt had encouraged. She became a dear companion to Blunt, who praised her artistic skill and friendship many times. As his health deteriorated, Brasier urged me to visit without delay.

Blunt's wit never diminished, and I will cite only a few examples. At the front door of his cottage, to the side of the Watts Gallery, was the warning, "Beware of the Scolo-pendrium!"—*Asplenium scolopendrium*, or hart's-tongue fern, to the cognoscente. During my visit, another guest appeared, and an amusing discussion ensued about art-works depicting cherubs, embellished by the ridiculous ways in which they might be categorized in a museum. He once sent a very funny letter, a parody of that "regrettable introduction from the States," the Christmas letter.

Of Flowers & a Village shows Blunt's wit on nearly every page, along with abundant commentary on flower lore, gar-deners, and botanists. The villagers of Dewbury, all associ-ated in some way with flowers, are mostly a colorful lot, capturing the British eccentricity beloved by Americans. Written in the form of rambling letters from a Wilfrid Sharp to his goddaughter for most of one year, there is probably more truth here than fiction. Blunt—I mean *Sharp*—takes the occasion to deliver little botanical lectures and to ex-press his opinion on a number of issues from flower arrang-ing to botanical taxonomy. Perhaps I've revealed too much already. Enjoy this trifle, as have I, and read a few letters each evening—if you can stop at only a few!

JAMES J. WHITE

Curator of Art & Principal Research Scholar
Hunt Institute for Botanical Documentation
Carnegie Mellon University
Pittsburgh, Pennsylvania

Of Flowers & a Village

Facsimile of the original edition of 1963

Of Flowers

&

a Village

An Entertainment for Flower Lovers

BY
WILFRID BLUNT

Illustrated by
RICHARD SHIRLEY SMITH

HAMISH HAMILTON
LONDON

'Offer'd as small Pills made up of sundry Herbs, and gilt with a certain brightness of Stile; in the choice whereof I have not much labour'd, but took them as they came to Hand . . .'

ABRAHAM COWLEY
Of Plants

I could, as others, [have] made use of such words, as few would have understood, and in a Pedantick style, pretended to mighty matters, which, when rightly considered, would have proved just nothing: But I hate such arrogancy, and proud foolery . . .

JOHN RAE, *Flora*
To the Reader
Second Impression, 1676

Acknowledgments

Permission to quote is gratefully acknowledged to: Longmans, Green and Co. and the late Sir Jagadis Bose (*Plant Autographs*); Laurence Pollinger Ltd. and the Estate of the late Mrs. Frieda Lawrence (passage from a work by D. H. Lawrence); George Allen and Unwin Ltd. and Professor W. O. James (*Background to Gardening*); Faber and Faber Ltd. and Mr. N. Leslie Cave (*The Iris*); The Medici Society Ltd. and the late Eleanour Sinclair Rohde (*The Scented Garden*); G. Bell and Sons Ltd. and Sir Edward Salisbury (*The Living Garden*); and Thomas Nelson and Sons Ltd. and the late Reginald Farrer (*The English Rock-Garden*).

Author's Note

I BELIEVE it is customary, in a work of fiction, for the author to declare that all the characters in it are wholly imaginary. Of the principal characters in this book this is true of all but two. Those who are fortunate enough to know 'Delia' will probably recognize her; but she must not be held responsible for all of Delia's remarks and actions. Nor can I deny that Wilfrid Sharp bears a certain superficial resemblance to Wilfrid Blunt, though the latter hastens to dissociate himself from some of the quite outrageous opinions held by the former. But I particularly wish to stress that no reference is intended to any other past or present inhabitant of Compton or its neighbourhood. I repeat: this book is *fiction*.

The letters are dated with day and month, but no year is given; it may, however, be assumed that they were written around 1960. I have little doubt that an ingenious, leisured and hostile reader would be able, by reference to blizzards, droughts, leap-years, the fall of Western and Orthodox Easter, the date of the theft of the Goya from the National Gallery, and so on, to establish that there were no possible years in which they *could* have been written; should he succeed in doing so, it will not greatly worry me.

As for Flora—she is not, of course, intended to be more than a plain peg upon which to hang a few stray botanical and horticultural reflections seasoned with village gossip, and I have deliberately left her unpainted and unvarnished.

I am afraid that I have allowed myself what, to mix my metaphors, might be described as a few leg-pulls at the soft under-bellies of the botanists. I hope they will forgive me, for many of them are my friends and many have shown me much kindness. But I do feel that, as an outsider, I may possibly be in a position to see one or two things in better perspective than they can. I have tried to write in the same spirit as did Dr. Renier, that Anglophile Dutchman who, in his *The English, are they human?*, poked kindly fun at what seemed to him absurd in the English way of life. Perhaps I shall provoke a botanist to write a book about the follies of schoolmasters; if so, I will gladly provide him with 'copy'.

I have, as always, to thank many friends. Mrs. Robert Gere, Mrs. Arthur Harrison, Mrs. Hubert Hartley, the late Mrs. George Sargeaunt, Miss Ruth Verner, Mr. Raef Payne, Mr. Maurice Percival, Mr. Patrick Synge and Mr. Francis Thompson very kindly read the typescript and made most valuable suggestions. Dr. John Gilmour, Mr. John Holmstrom and Mr. Igor Vinogradoff were among the many who helped me on points of detail. To Mr. Richard Shirley Smith

I am particularly indebted for his delightful illustrations and dust jacket. Once again Miss V. Thayre did the typing with her customary speed and accuracy, and the Hon. Mrs. Mackinnon very kindly checked the page proofs.

W.J.W.B.

The Watts Gallery
Compton
Guildford
March 31st 1963

SEPTEMBER

My dear Flora,

Only a godfather who is on the fringes of senility would have overlooked your birthday (the twenty-third, wasn't it?) of at least a month ago; I've no excuse to offer, except that I've been pretty busy. But I've now asked Wallace and Barr to send you a dozen martagon lilies. I think you ought to be able to naturalize them in that piece of rough grass beyond the peonies; they grow wild, I see, 'from Monmouthshire to the borders of Mongolia', so they ought to be pretty accommodating. I'm delighted to hear your mother has agreed to let you have that part of the garden to yourself. You'll find it easier to endure her summer bedding and monster herbaceous plants if you've a corner where you can grow what you like.

And now I'll tell you why I've been so busy: I've found a house! To be more accurate, I've found a *garden*, and am proposing to make the best of a house that isn't ideal. The place is called Orchards, and it's in Dewbury, an incredibly remote little village yet actually only about four miles from Dorking.

To get the house over first. It's harmless, featureless, 1800-stock-brick and rather larger than I'd intended. But the rooms are nice, and there's nowhere where a man even of my height can bump his head. (I'd never have tolerated those medieval death-traps—not even for such a garden: short people have no notion what the tall have to suffer. I can still hear my aunt saying cheerfully as I crashed into her Elizabethan beam for the tenth time, 'That sounds like your funny old head again!') Really the only objection to the house is a negative one: its lack of character. Externally this is partly disguised by a *Magnolia grandiflora*, and I think I've enough treasures and bric-à-brac to make the inside passable.

But the garden! It was laid out, sixty or so years ago, by someone who really knew his job; and though it's been hideously neglected latterly by Trotter (my predecessor), there's almost nothing important that's beyond recovery. Including the orchard and wood there are nearly three acres of it. The trees are magnificent—many of them unusual and one or two quite rare (there's a splendid davidia). The tulip-tree is one of the several hundred that claim to be the largest in England; no doubt they were all planted at the same time, and it's certainly much older than the present house. The eucalyptuses are so rampant that I could almost keep Koala bears. By the front door there's a seven-foot-high rosemary—which would appear to give the lie to the medieval legend that it never grows taller than the height of Christ when He was on earth.

The general design is quite excellent. There are stone steps and good garden ornaments and a yew walk. (I'm sorry if I write like a house agent's advertisement, but I want to give you the facts). There's a small stream, and perhaps there's a touch of lime here and there in the soil because no one in the village seems to have rhododendrons (yet *Magnolia stellata* flourishes). Of course there's an appalling amount of resuscitation to be done; but now than I'm a man of leisure, it's exactly the sort of challenge I'm looking for. As to neighbours—I've a colonel to right of me and a colonel to left of me, but both nicely camouflaged by trees. This must be one of the last places left in Surrey where one can find retired colonels and no rhododendrons.

I won't bore you with more details, because I'm determined to take you over to see it all and to pick your brains. Would you be free next Saturday? If so, I'd collect you at Kingsmead about midday. We could stop for lunch on the way (I know of a place near Godstone where you can get a most excellent meal), and I'd get you back in time for dinner—to which, perhaps, your mother might like to invite me. Do say Yes.

My love to your parents.

Ever your very affectionate godfather

Wilfrid Sharp

September 20th　　　　　　　　　Orchards
　　　　　　　　　　　　　Dewbury, nr. Dorking

I'm so pleased that you liked the glimpse you had of
Orchards; You know I have the highest opinion of your
taste and judgment. Plump little Mrs. Benham has done
wonders in the house (she really looks like being the
perfect housekeeper) and has now 'given permission'—
for that's what it amounts to, these days—for me to have
my first guest to stay in October. I hope it will be *you*; I
badly need more advice about the garden. Trotter (I
gather) was a 'nature-lover': that's to say, he let the garden go hang and rushed about with a gun killing things.
Then, as I think I told you, the gun went off by accident
and killed *him*.

So will you come? Any time soon after October 1st
would be all right; I imagine you'll be back from Scotland by then. And you must stay at least a week. The

leaves are just beginning to turn, and the country is looking lovely. I always wanted to live in the country and 'commute'; but it wouldn't have suited Betty, who thought that civilization stopped at Hampstead. I wonder if you have remembered that it's five years today since Betty died. I know how fond of her you were, and I shan't ever forget your kindness to her during her last illness. How different everything might have been for us if Jonathan had lived. . . . But I must stop being melancholy, and count my many blessings.

Incidentally, I'm delighted to find that Mrs. Benham likes flowers, though she has declined the offer of a small corner of garden for herself: 'Flowers,' she announced, 'just don't *percolate* for me!' Her horticultural vocabulary is altogether peculiar: she told me that in her last post the house was full of 'happy asters', which from her description must have been hippeastrums, and that the 'mongolia' was much bigger than mine. She also showed me a pressed 'idle vice' that her sister brought her back from Switzerland. Oh yes—and best of all: 'Camellia? Now isn't that the flower that's always changing colour?'

Which reminds me that you always spell 'camellia' wrong; the mispronunciation is so firmly established that lots of people do. Old Sir Sydney Cockerell told me that he once won a penny in Kew Gardens off the Archbishop of Canterbury (Lang), who had wagered that it had only one 'l'. I wonder when and why the pronunciation went wrong; probably, I suppose, because of 'Ophelia', 'Amelia', 'lobelia' and so on. That incurable optimist Fowler (*Modern English Usage*) believes that when the spelling becomes better known, people will get the pronunciation right. I very much doubt it: his campaign for calling eschscholtzia 'isho'ltsia' has been a dead failure—except, I believe, with the Americans. I see that George Kamel (Latinized as Camellus) was a Moravian Jesuit who travelled in Asia at the end of the seventeenth century.

I wonder whether the Archbishop could spell 'dahlia'. Since it was named after the Swedish botanist Dahl, and since there's another plant called a dalea (named after Samuel Dale), there seems no possible excuse for making 'dahlia' rhyme (approximately) with 'failure'—'an ignorant conceit, a piece of affected Cockneyism' as someone wrote in 1836. But there's nothing to be done about it now, and even Fowler refuses to champion so lost a cause.

Enough of this lecture! Give my love to your aunt and tell her that I still remember my Edinburgh Festival with great pleasure.

September 26th

All is prepared, and I'll meet you at Dorking on Monday—no, I mean Monday week—at 3.40. I'm very sorry to hear you haven't been well, and I hope the specialist will give you a good report. At all events, don't let him do anything to make you postpone your visit. By the way, I've found a most enchanting neighbour, a Mrs. Lovell who is longing to meet you. If you don't fall for her at sight I'll never ask you here again!

I've great plans for the garden and am longing to discuss them with you. I propose putting a dozen large tubs on the terrace in front of the loggia and stuffing them with every bright and sweet-smelling thing I can find. Then two large beds for precious plants that Ovenden won't be allowed to touch; that will still leave me with plenty of lawn. Then shrubs, old roses . . . I won't go on: much easier to show you on the spot. But before all else, of course, I've got to clear the jungle that has swallowed up the paved walk, the flowerbeds, the— well, *everything*! Trotter's neglect was absolutely criminal.

Oh! I looked up *Iris histrioides* for you in Dykes. *Histrioides* means 'like *histrio*', and *histrio* means (as I ought to have remembered) an actor. The name was given (to *I. histrio*), says Dykes, 'because the flower is so gaily painted': a strange choice! But, as you will doubtless have discovered already, the ways of the botanists are often incomprehensible.

I've just sent off a mammoth order for daffodil and

other bulbs. While making out my list I came, by chance, across a 1939 catalogue and was horrified to see how some of the prices had risen. For example, Pheasant's Eye narcissi, for which I then paid ninepence a dozen, are now eight shillings: i.e. almost ten times as much. If I complain, I shall no doubt be told that I am getting an 'improved' form; and if I say I don't *want* an improved form, but just the little wildling from the Swiss pastures, which is so abundant that it ought practically to be given away—I shall be considered mad.

Mrs. Benham has now revealed her first Achilles heel: she is *maddeningly* radio-active in the kitchen, and plays the wretched thing full blast.

All other news when we meet.

Ever your very affectionate godfather

Wilfrid Sharp

OCTOBER

October 1st

My very dear Flora,

I can't *begin* to tell you how distressed I am. I simply *can't* believe it. *Of course* the right thing is to get a second opinion; I've always heard that Arbuthnot was by far the best man in the country on all these spinal troubles, and perhaps he will say that it isn't as bad as you fear. I just can't bear to think of you on your back for months on end.

Were you well enough to travel, I would suggest your seeing a Swiss or German specialist; I have tremendous faith in them. There is a Dr. Schwabe in Zürich who has worked miracles, I believe. But from what you say, I'm afraid that that would be quite out of the question. I would most gladly pay the fee if Arbuthnot wanted to fly anyone over.

I won't write more now—I don't feel like writing about trivialities at the moment. I know you'll tell me as soon as you get Arbuthnot's report and I *do* so hope he'll say that the whole thing is nonsense.

October 5th

O my *very* dear Flora, this is *bitter* news!

I had been hoping against hope that Arbuthnot would make a different diagnosis. Yet I'm thankful that they've told you all the facts. Now you know how you stand, and you've the courage to face the months ahead. At least you have the promise of an almost complete recovery. And fortunately you've so many interests. Think of all the books you'll now have time to read! I'll keep you supplied with whatever you want, so just let me know—when you feel up to it. I too at last have leisure, and I'll write to you regularly and tell you what I'm reading, and thinking, and doing in the garden. And I'll try to send you flowers that will stand that long journey. I do wish you weren't going to be so far away; but if Edinburgh can give you the most up-to-date treatment, then obviously you must stay there—even when you are well enough to be moved.

David is coming over next week. I won't pretend he'll be a full substitute for his sister, but I'm looking forward to seeing him; I expect I shall be a bit lonely here at first. Your mother rang up to say she was thinking of cancelling the party for the silver wedding, but I know you wouldn't wish this. I hope your father will be able to talk her round.

I looked in at the office last week and found they were getting on splendidly without me. It's a fatal mistake to believe that one is indispensable! But they greeted me with the greatest cordiality, pretended that they needed my advice on some new mining shares, and begged me to look in whenever I was around.

October 10th

So you are safely installed, your mother says! I'm very sorry there's so much clatter without and so much chatter within; yet I can't help thinking that you'll get used to both, and perhaps in time even be rather grateful for the latter. Really there's a lot to be said for a public ward.

And talking of chatter, do you know this: 'I think the presence of human beings in large numbers is fatiguing to plants; perhaps they are sensitive to the sound of human voices'? Colette wrote it, and isn't it nice?

But is it true? Certainly no one could call your mother a silent woman, yet she can keep a cyclamen alive in the house for months—which is more than I can do. I wonder if the subject has ever been scientifically investigated.

For example, why do plants do better, in general, in the country than in the town? Because there's better air, better soil, less wanton damage? Or because there are fewer people and less noise? Why does the almond flourish in London? Because it's able to absorb moisture —or whatever it is it needs—through smoke-grimed leaves more successfully than other trees? Or because it happens to be gregarious and rather hard of hearing?

> Speak not, whisper not,
> Here bloweth thyme and bergamot.

For perhaps if we speak, or even whisper, they'll stop blowing.

Incidentally, any flower that can stand up to the noise of the aeroplanes here deserves a Royal Horticultural Society's Award of Merit. For some reason or other, the day I came over to view the house there wasn't a murmur in the skies; I now discover that there is a large aerodrome only three miles away—which probably explains why the house was so cheap.

I've got the builders here, adding to the kitchen which has turned out to be too small; it's a pity it wasn't done before I moved in, because it's making life difficult for Mrs. Benham. In fact, I might have had to postpone your visit in any case. How nice builders are! Or perhaps I've been lucky. There are three men and a youth, all cheerful and hard-working in every kind of weather. 'I won't 'urt that rose,' said the bricklayer; 'I've got a garden of my own.' And he promised me a slip of a saxifrage that I'd never heard of. 'Got an award with it last year,' he told me. 'Where?' I asked; 'at the village show?' 'No, at Vincent Square.' Isn't that rather splendid? I've promised to fetch the plant and meet 'the Missus and the kids.' But is it really impossible for a man to lay a brick nowadays without blasting hideous noises from a transistor wireless? His saxifrage must certainly be stone-deaf.

Yesterday five sheep got into the garden and did quite a bit of damage. It's very annoying, but the farmer seems a nice chap and I don't want to start by quarrelling with him. However, he had better take care: old Parkinson warmly recommends the boiled shank-bones of sheep for edging flower-beds.

October 17th

Even after what I'd heard on all sides, I was astonished when your mother told me that Mrs. Lovell, whom you've never even met and I barely know, had sent you some flowers. I've been meaning to tell you about her—because she's unique, and the first thing I want to do when you're on your feet again is to get you here to meet her.

I really don't see where to begin. You know how some people, at the very moment of first meeting, radiate either warmth or an icy blast? I don't think I've ever before had a stronger sensation of sheer warmheartedness than when I first met Mrs. Lovell. She lives in what everyone calls 'the other big house in the village', Mrs. Puttenham (whom I've not yet encountered) occupying the Manor. Mrs. Lovell's house is in fact a good three-quarters of a mile from the village proper, and it isn't particularly big—a pleasant rambling

Regency house that really wants a lot of money spending on it. Mrs. Lovell is Scottish, but you could sooner find her house in Ireland.

She is, I suppose, a bit younger than I am—say about fifty-five: tall and bigly built, with greying auburn hair, prominent cheek-bones and rather high colouring. Her voice is wonderfully soft and musical, yet her speech is clipped and staccato. Perhaps the most improbable thing about her is her handwriting: you would expect a large, sprawling 'Ouida' hand; in fact she has a tiny gothic script like that of a thirteenth-century Bible. I enclose a letter she has just sent me (and which I would like back), partly for the writing, and partly to show you how charmingly she writes to an almost complete stranger.

You can't picture Mrs. Lovell without her dogs—two golden retrievers called 'Hither' and 'Thither'. (I don't, as you know, much care for dogs—and still less for 'twee' names for them: they work such havoc in the garden; but these are winners). Nor without her flowers: because there seemed, although it's October, to be flowers everywhere. The house is glorious—all the stuffs and colours *exactly* right, but rather faded and dog-chewed; I've been told that at the Manor everything is brand-new, expensive and hideous. And she has one lovely picture—a 'Madonna and Child', attributed to a rather nebulous Flemish artist known as the Master of the Madonna of the Overturned Beehive.

Mrs. Lovell asked me to tea and a Miss Parker was there too—a retired schoolmistress I gather, and very talkative; but I had eyes and ears for no one but Mrs.

Lovell, and I can hardly wait for you to meet her. Mr. Lovell works in London during the week and I haven't seen him yet; I'm told he's just as nice as she is. What luck to find such people here!

As I was leaving, Mrs. Lovell whispered to me, 'Mr. Sharp, do please be *perfectly* sweet to Helen Parker; she's had a *terribly* sad life. . . .' But how or why I don't yet know, for Miss Parker joined us at that moment and I couldn't get the rest.

I got home to find a note from Mrs. Benham on the hall table: 'Flocks is in the garden.' But it wasn't more sheep: only various *Phlox subulata* that I'd ordered from a nurseryman in Dorking.

In the evenings, when I can tear myself away from my new TV set, I've been reading about von Frisch's experiments with bees. Using bits of variously coloured and toned papers he proved that bees are colour-blind to red, though not to yellow or blue. Then why are they so fond of red corn-poppies? Because the corn-poppy reflects not only red rays, invisible to bees, but ultra-violet rays visible to bees but not to us. The part of the spectrum visible to bees is further in the direction of the violet than ours, cutting out the red and including the ultra-violet. There's an explanation for everything if one only knows where to look.

Very glad to hear that you are becoming reconciled to captivity. It's wonderful that you're able to move your right leg a bit; a doctor friend of mine tells me that this is a *most* hopeful sign that that leg, at any rate, may get completely back to normal quite quickly. Let me know

when you need books, but I gather from your mother
that you aren't really up to reading yet.

Enclosure

The Pond House

October 16th   Dewbury

Dear Mr. Sharp

I do not expect to call you this very long, but I am so
conventional that I do so now.

It is delightful that you have come to live here and
don't play bridge, or have a wife or anything tiresome,
and have pockets full of seeds.

Shall you like to dine with us on Tuesday? Dead
quiet, unless Miss Parker plays the piano. Only her &
us and you & a godchild who has run away from school
& one misanthropic publisher & oh—Mrs. Waller. She
is 89 and Irish & so fragile that please do not sneeze.

Thistledown wd. be a ton of coals to her.

Yours sincerely

Delia Lovell

C

October 21st

I must say a word about my Colonels and their 'womenfolk', who on the whole have been kind and welcoming.

Colonel Stringer is straight from the pages of a pre-First-War *Punch*—a cocksure little man who knows what's wrong with the Army, the Navy, the Air Force, the Government and the Church of England. What is wrong is simply that there isn't Colonel Stringer, or someone exactly like Colonel Stringer, at the top. His wife is gentle and banal and still pretty. Her conversation consists mostly of remarks such as, 'I always think the food you get in restaurants isn't as good as what you get at home', or, 'I always think that Christmas is so *tiring*'. These pronouncements she makes with the air of one who, after profound thought, has hit upon a great

truth not previously revealed to mankind. She agrees
with her husband in everything, and regrets as much as
he does that he doesn't run England. They have a large
green mongrel dog (it really *is* almost green!) that barks
incessantly and is on the way to becoming a considerable nuisance in my garden.

Colonel Moon is tall, distinguished-looking, silent.
Mrs. Moon I actively dislike. She has outsize nostrils
and a raucous voice. I spotted her at once as one of those
domineering women whom one must immediately hit,
and hit hard, if one is not to go under. You remember
what Goethe said about everyone being born to become
either a hammer or an anvil? Mrs. Moon is a sledge-
hammer, and I, till I pulled myself together, was one of
Nature's anvils. She came round to Orchards and said,
'Mr. Sharp, you probably know that Mrs. Trotter—
poor dear, I feel so sorry for her!—did the church
flowers in Advent, so I've put your name down to take
over from her—or rather to provide the flowers, and no
doubt Mrs. Benham would arrange them.' 'Then you
can take a large piece of indiarubber and rub it out
again,' I said. No—to be honest, I didn't: that was
what I wanted to say. But I refused—not because I've
the slightest objection to providing the flowers, but because I don't propose to be treated like that by Mrs.
Moon or by anyone else. I may be a worm—but I've
turned. When it comes (as inevitably it will) to bazaars,
Conservative fêtes, charity concerts, outings for the deaf
and collections for the Melanesian Mission—I'm told
she finds an outlet for her bossiness (and quite genuine

goodness) in running everything—I think I shall be treated with more consideration.

This morning I met Delia (as I'm to call her) walking down the village clutching a large medicine-bottle and surrounded by dogs. I asked her if she were ill (nobody could have looked healthier). 'No, Darling'—apparently she calls everyone 'darling'—'I'm terribly well. I'm only taking some medicine to old Mrs. Peters. Actually it's brandy, and—Darling!—isn't it fascinating? she's never had brandy before in her life and she *really* thinks it's medicine!' She showed me the label she had written —so small that I can't imagine that Mrs. Peters (the butcher's mother) will be able to read it: 'One table-spoonful to be taken twice daily after meals.'

'Let Besodeiah rejoice with the Nettle,' wrote mad Kit Smart two hundred years ago in his *Jubilate Agno*. But not me: later this morning, while tipping rubbish, I tripped and fell into a bed of them! No great damage done, but it was undignified and unpleasant.

I expect you know the French couplet:

> Cet animal est très méchant:
> Quand on l'attaque, il se défend.

Substitute 'ce végétal' for 'cet animal' and you have my views on the subject. 'The nettle,' as one of the old Herbalists so truly said, 'may be found by feeling on the darkest night.'

I brought a bit of nettle back to the house and studied it and got some books out. I somehow felt I'd get my own back on it if I found out its secrets: also a sort of homœopathic cure, perhaps. It seems that each of those innocent-looking hairs is nothing more nor less than a hypodermic syringe charged with formic acid to poison and something else to inflame the wound. The glass-sharp nozzle of the syringe snaps at an angle, so that it can spike one more easily, and the poisons are packed into a resilient little balloon so that pressure will drive them into the wound. And this devilry is designed to last: when the Natural History Museum was bombed during the Second World War, one of the botanists who was helping to carry the herbarium specimens to safety was stung by a nettle pressed by Linnaeus 200 years earlier!

We've got two native nettles. A third—the Roman nettle—is said to have been introduced here by the Romans, who grew it 'to rubbe and chafe their limbs, when through extreame cold they should be stiffe and benummed' in our inclement climate: a pleasant but an improbable story.

I was surprised to discover that the hop is a member of the nettle family; and so also until recently (for it's now been shifted) was the elm, and I believe sensitive skins can feel the sting of the hairs of an elm-leaf.

We're lucky in Europe: some of the Asiatic nettles are highly dangerous, and the 'mealum-ma'—the great shrubby nettle of northern India, a plant the size of an apple-tree—is almost a killer. Sir Joseph Hooker had the greatest difficulty in getting natives to help him cut one down, and though he didn't actually get stung, 'the scentless effluvium was so powerful that mucous matter poured from my eyes and nose all the rest of the afternoon'. But a French botanist, Leschenault, gives a terrifying account of the pain of the sting—like being rubbed with a red-hot iron. Then his jaw went stiff and he thought he'd got lockjaw. He was very ill for nearly a fortnight, but ultimately recovered.

The Nepchas (whoever they may be) are said to use branches of mealum-ma to whip their sons with; I suppose the boys become more or less immunized in time.

Now the sting of the mealum-ma is much worse in autumn than at any other season. Do you suppose that Nepcha youth is exceptionally wicked in September? There must be some reason for it.

Do these botanical lectures bore you? If so, let me know and I'll stop them at once and merely feed you with village gossip. But I thought they might give you something to think about while you're in bed, and now that I'm alone in the country I rather enjoy having someone to tell what I've been reading about. I hope the massage is doing good; I'm afraid the exercises must be rather tiring, but it's an excellent sign that you're able to do them at all.

I shall look forward to getting a first-hand account of you from your mother as soon as she is back. I thought she was looking very tired when I last saw her, and perhaps the break will do her good. If only she could learn to *relax*, how much better it would be for everyone—including your father. She tells me that Doris has given notice, and really, to be quite honest, I'm not at all surprised.

October 25th

Dinner with Delia was great fun, and my only disappointment was that Humphrey (her husband) wasn't there; but I'm to meet him soon. Miss Parker didn't play the piano: just as well, perhaps, as I think that anything louder than Couperin on a clavichord would have disintegrated old Mrs. Waller. It seems that Mrs. Waller was, in her day, a dashing explorer and the first Englishwoman to cross the Atacama desert; now, poor dear, she daren't cross the road unaided. The publisher was so busy taking pills—blue before dinner, yellow with the fish; and two red ones at the end of the meal— that he had little time for conversation. The goddaughter was incredibly pretty and hadn't really run away from school—just an exeat to attend a sister's wedding.

Your mother came over on Wednesday and brought me an excellent report of you; and she was full of praise of the young house surgeon. But within five minutes of her arrival we had quarrelled—no, that's rather too strong a word: 'failed to see eye to eye'—about lawns. She took one look at mine and said she'd give me, for Christmas, some new-fangled contraption or other that scraped, fertilized and weed-killed simultaneously, and was guaranteed to turn the worst lawn in the world into a billiard-table in six months. She hinted that it was extremely expensive, but that she simply couldn't bear to see a piece of grass looking like that.

I thanked her very much, but told her what she must know already—that I liked my lawn pretty well as it was; it's almost the only thing in the garden that wasn't wholly neglected by the Trotters. I said I didn't want it turned into a soulless strip of green plastic. I liked the daisies and the thyme and all the little nameless plants that gave it character and texture. I even liked the moss. I proposed to eliminate the plantains, but that wouldn't involve the use of expensive machinery. I hinted that I'd far rather have two or three camellias for tubs.

She was annoyed. You know how she always says she likes people to 'have the courage of their convictions'. I find, however, that what she really wants is for them to have the courage of *her* convictions! She said, 'Your lawn isn't grass. A lawn means grass.'

'Now there you're on very dangerous ground,' I told her. 'Shakespeare's lawns, Milton's lawns, were forest glades. That "lawn" equals "grass" is a modern corruption, and I'd be prepared to bet that before Mr. Edwin Bunning invented the lawn-mower in 1831, it was an impossibility. I don't suppose it was even possible until the introduction of selective weed-killers. You'd never have passed Francis Bacon's "finely shorn" grass. Don't you like the scythed grass of continental gardens? The English lawn is so terribly English: so respectable, so bourgeois, so *dull*. The velvet lawn is as suburban as the "white" shirt we're always being urged to achieve by some washing powder or other. I'd keep my lawn scythed —if only I could find anyone these days who could do it properly.'

At this your mother went all patriotic. She implied that the English lawn, like Shakespeare and the monarchy, was a sacred institution. 'It takes 300 years to make a real English lawn,' she added.

'In that case,' I said, 'it's rather late for me to start now. But I thought you told me that your machine could do it in six months.'

I won't bore you with the rest. It was clear that she thought me stupid, pig-headed, ungrateful and—worst of all—un-English. (I wonder whether she knows that for bowling-greens a New Zealand grass is now always used.) Much though I love her, I couldn't help thinking that if I had married her we would have got on each other's nerves a good deal. I don't think I shall get my camellias now!

Consider your mother's lawn. Heaven knows what she spends a year on lawn sand, sulphate of iron, sulphur of potash, dried blood, Verdone, Velvaz, Supertox, DDT (for—or rather, against—leatherjackets) and all the rest. Then, machine or no machine, there are the hours and hours of labour (at five or six shillings an hour). And what's the result? Whenever I visit Kingsmead I find the lawn being 'treated', and half covered with fertilizer or fungicide. She begs you to come and see it in two months time, and you do, and what do you find? That some new patent moss-killer has taken possession of it! I hope, and believe, that you're on my side about this, and agree with me that a lawn ought to look as though God, and not Messrs. —, had made it.

Incidentally, I see that W. H. Hudson also supports me; indeed he goes even further than I do: 'I am not a lover of lawns,' he wrote. 'Rather would I see daisies in their thousands, ground ivy, hawkweed, and even the hated plantain with tall stems, and dandelions with splendid flowers and fairy down, than a too-well-tended lawn.' As for William Robinson, author of the famous *English Flower Garden*—well, he simply wants a meadow: 'Who would not rather see the waving grass with countless flowers than a close-shaven surface without a blossom? Imagine the labour wasted in this ridiculous plan of cutting the heads off flowers and grass.'

I've been to sherry with the Moons, and my first reaction—that the Colonel is a charmer and his wife a shocker—was confirmed. The most remarkable thing about the Moons' drawing-room is that practically nothing in it can be directly used for the purpose for which it was intended. The piano is covered with photographs and would take a quarter of an hour to open, when it would doubtless prove to be out of tune. On the piano stool stands a fern in a pot on a mat on a cloth on another cloth. It is clear that flowers may never be put in the vases. A sherry-glass may not be placed direct on an occasional table; under it there must be two mats—a rough mat, and then a soft mat to prevent the rough mat from scratching the table. Chairs and sofas have faded slip-on cotton covers to protect the real covers. The general impression the room gives is that the owners have been away and haven't had time to 'open up' since they got back. Delia, who has seen Mrs. Moon's bedroom, says that the bedside mats are wrapped in cellophane.

Delia also tells me that Mrs. Moon has a 'boutique' in Dorking, full of lamp-shades and table-mats made out of old title-deeds and flower-prints. She herself never appears behind the counter, I gather; when 'the girl' decamped at very short notice, Colonel Moon was rushed in to hold the fort.

The addition to the kitchen is nearly finished, and I shall miss my brick-layer, who is a joy. He came up to me when I was hacking back some laurels, and I said something about not liking to have to mutilate trees. He replied, 'God gave us 'air, but that don't mean 'e means us to wear it 'alf way down our backs.'

I'm glad you'll let me send you from time to time the by-products of my reading—yes, I promise not to write about politics or the world situation. I am (as Abraham Cowley said of himself) 'but a Pigmy in Learning, and scarce sufficient to express the Virtues of the vile Sea-Weed. . . . Yet wherefore should I not attempt?' Wherefore not indeed!

October 29th

I've been re-reading the Memoirs of Babar, the first
Mughal Emperor, and I see that he too had the right
ideas about lawns. Of the Garden of Fidelity, one of the
gardens that he made around Kabul, he wrote in October 1519: 'It was looking its best. *Its lawns were one
sheet of clover* [my italics], its pomegranate trees a glorious yellow and the fruit hanging red on the branches....'

Babar had marvellous sensibility. He could write of
an apple-tree in late autumn, 'On each of its branches
five or six scattered leaves still remained, exhibiting a
beauty which the painter with all his skill, might attempt
in vain to portray.' He could interrupt a journey in the
Hindu Kush to collect tulips—'thirty-three different
kinds' including a 'hundred-petalled' one (which must
have been a double poppy) and one that smelt like a
rose. Miniatures show him directing the planting of
roses and narcissi, his favourite flowers. But he was a

child of his age: after an unsuccessful attempt had been made to poison him he wrote quite unconcernedly, 'I ordered the taster to be cut in pieces, the cook to be flayed alive, and one of the women to be trampled to death by an elephant. . . .'

Having, thanks to those nettles, become involved in the hostility of plants, I've now been reading further. I find that Nature, though she sometimes uses a gun, doesn't much use it in anger (I'll tell you more of this another day). Her principal weapons are the sword, stiletto, bayonet, saw, javelin and harpoon.

Sometimes she seems to be almost unnecessarily lavish with her armoury. Don't you think that gorse, armed cap-à-pie like a medieval knight, looks a bit ridiculous? Sometimes she's a bit mean, not usually bothering to put prickles on the upper leaves of a tall holly because they're out of reach of browsing animals (have you ever noticed that?).

Cacti and their relations are her last word in defensive armour, and they need every bit of protection that they can get. In South America at the height of a drought you can see wild asses picking at the bases of the melocacti—which look like vegetable porcupines—trying to uproot them so that they can get at the juicy tissues at the point of least defence.

Prickly pears have bristles that are devilishly barbed, as I know to my cost; and the dasylirion has leaves as sharp as saws. We mayn't have these growing wild in England, nor the American poison ivy (which the Munich Botanic Gardens keep in a cage like a lion at the Zoo), but we've our fair share of lesser torments—thistles, brambles, wild roses and so on. We've killers like the fly agaric, water hemlock and deadly nightshade, and in our greenhouses there are primulas which give some people a nasty rash.

Nature's defence systems seem mostly to have been erected against the lower animals. Man has axes and secateurs and gardening-gloves, weed-killers and wiles. He may get pricked; but he does get blackberries.

To turn to quite a different subject: isn't it odd that one can't call a flower 'good-looking'? The O.E.D. defines the word as 'having an attractive, beautiful, pretty or handsome appearance', so don't you think we might add it to the limited vocabulary of floral praise? 'Well-dressed' also, perhaps, and no doubt you'll be able to think of many more. The wine merchants, with their 'clever little hocks' and 'intellectual Sauternes', have enormously enlarged the vinous vocabulary—and, I think, unreasonably, because all that most people can honestly say about a wine is that it's drinkable or undrinkable.

I don't know about you, but personally I find myself using—quite irrationally, of course—human standards when assessing the good looks of flowers. There was a music hall song of my childhood—something, I think, about

> Pretty little Pansy faces
> Looking o'er the garden wall . . .

I pictured pansies six feet tall, smiling rather podgily

and not unlike Cook: benign, but certainly not good-looking.

What plants could reasonably be called 'good-looking', then? Not the cypripediums with their underhung Hapsburg jaws, the pouting snapdragons, the grotesque Cape pondweed with flowers like false teeth on the ends of a pencil, the stapelias clearly made out of odds and ends by the Women's Institute, the shoddily designed little rhodohypoxis or the bloated calceolarias. Not even the sweet-peas, those *jolies-laides* with *retroussé* charms. Perhaps a perfectly formed rose or camellia is the answer.

And well-dressed? The colchicum and *Amaryllis belladonna* are naked; the lilac and mock-orange are hopelessly overdressed. But don't you think some of the hellebores—*Helleborus corsicus*, for instance—have learned the art of dressing well?

Things are rather chaotic here at the moment. Mrs. Benham announced coyly at breakfast that she was 'having trouble with the Minister of the Interior'—a euphemism, new to me, for a belly-ache—and has now taken to her bed. Then Ovenden—oh, how I dislike his red hair and beard!—shuffled in, much bandaged, to tell me that he'd sprained his thumb. (I have the feeling that Ovenden's thumb is always going to trouble him when there's any hard or distasteful work in view; it isn't as though he were an old man—he's quite a bit younger than I am.) So it doesn't look as if I'll be able to get the place properly tidied up before the winter— and now we seem to be in for a spell of wet weather too. But I love the smell of dank leaves, and the sound of rain beating on the windows. I wish you were here at the moment, sitting in front of my log fire and listening to Fischer-Dieskau singing 'Die Winterreise'. Are you terribly bored? If I don't ask much about your progress, it's only because I know that for the present there can be nothing more that you can tell me. I think you'd rather I just wrote about flowers or gossip.

And talking of gossip: poor Delia is in great distress. It appears that Mrs. Peters's enjoyment of her medicine wasn't quite so innocent as Delia had imagined, and the old lady has had a sharp attack of D.T. I find that Helen has known for some time that she drank; it was unfortunate that she hadn't happened to mention it to Delia.

P.S. I see that Robert Gathorne-Hardy compares the flowers of the Cape pondweed to 'miniature pink high-pooped boats'; I still think they're more like false teeth.

Ever your very affectionate godfather

Wilfrid Sharp

NOVEMBER

November 3rd

My dearest Flora,

It was *splendid* to get a letter in your own hand and to hear that you can now sit up in bed a bit. But *please* don't feel that my letters need answering; just a card from your aunt, now and then, to tell me how you are getting on, is all I ask for.

I've just been spending two days at Kew, working in the Library of the Herbarium. It was a sudden urge—from reading a book called *The Art of Botanical Illustration*, which made me think I'd like to look at some of the early herbals and other things; and the weather, which has made it impossible to work in the garden, settled it.

And talking of the weather, there's a charming misprint in the forecast this morning: 'Dry in moist parts of the British Isles'! Incidentally, have you noticed how hopelessly wrong the forecasts have been lately? Or are you like your dear mother—still full of trust, and very angry with anyone who refuses to trust with her? I'm quite prepared to believe it's impossible to predict the

weather with any reasonable hope of accuracy, even a
few hours ahead; but wouldn't it be nice if the prophets
occasionally admitted that they'd been mistaken! I expect
you've heard the story of Sir William Eden (Anthony
Eden's father) throwing his barometer out of the window and crying, 'There, you damned fool—see for
yourself!'

Your mother's weather-lore credulity has also always
fascinated me. She believes implicitly in St. Swithin's
forty days, in a good berry-year being followed by a
severe winter (the berries being Dame Nature's fore-
thought for the poor birds), and that two full moons in
the same month cause floods. I've heard her quote 'Fine
on Friday, fine on Sunday' in perfect seriousness; and,
as you probably remember, she discovers portents in
the behaviour of toads and snails, in the rising of fish,
the busyness of bees, the restlessness of cattle, the con-
gregating of crows, and so on. Statistics have, I need
hardly add, shown all this to be bunkum. I don't know
whether she insists upon her beans being sown under a
waning moon, but it wouldn't surprise me.

'The stock-in-trade of a weather prophet,' wrote
A. S. E. Ackermann, 'is of a slender and cheap description. He must have an inventive mind, a store of self-
confidence, an insensibility to ridicule, and, above all, a
keen memory for his successes and a prompt forgetful-
ness of his failures. He should by choice have a theory,
and this should be of the elastic order, so that if a predicted event does not punctually occur, he will be ready
with a sort of codicil to amend it.'

But to return to the Herbarium. I expect you know the building by sight—red eighteenth-century, near the main entrance to the Gardens, and looking as though it sheltered the humanities rather than science. But the tempo inside is more that of the ant-hill than of the cloister. There's a perpetual scurrying of feet—people coming and going between the Library and the Herbarium proper, which is a series of enormous echoing Victorian prisons stretching away behind the Georgian façade towards the mud-banks of the Thames.

Have you ever been inside a large herbarium? To a mere flower-lover it's one of the most depressing places imaginable—a sort of botanical cemetery with a million vegetable dead awaiting Judgment Day in their browned paper shrouds. It reeks of decay and dissolution. As I looked at its hundreds of little cells, each with its imprisoned botanist and his sheaf of plant folders, the whole place seemed to have so little to do with *flowers* that I found it almost possible to believe that old story —you probably know it—of the botanist who failed to recognize in the common daisy the familiar *Bellis perennis* of his *hortus siccus*. There was Benjamin Robinson, the American botanist, who when asked to identify a wild flower always replied, 'Press it, dry it, bring it back, and I'll name it for you'. I do so agree with Professor Dawson, who said: 'I hate Theology and Botany, but I love religion and flowers.'

But the botanists couldn't have been kinder. A man who, very possibly, was giving the best years of his life to 'lumping' a genus that his predecessor had given the best years of *his* life to 'splitting', cheerfully interrupted his work to find me some drawings by Ehret. (Do you know them? they're lovely.) It was doubly good of him, because from his point of view they were little more than 'pretty pictures'. Yes—one and all they were very helpful and charming. But to me they seemed as remote as Chinese, with a language all their own and values that I didn't share. I'm sure that if I'd said to one of them, 'In my left hand I've got a drawing by Rembrandt, and in my right a very small and dreary fungus unknown to science; which will you choose?' he'd have chosen the fungus.

I lunched at a small tea-place on the Green, decorated excruciatingly in orange and magenta. All the botanists go there, and being alone I could eaves-drop. One pair argued for nearly an hour as to which was the most suitable kind of water-cress to introduce into Trinidad. Two schoolmasters disagreeing about the umpire's decision in a house-match couldn't have got more heated. I suppose it simply amounts to this: that after a time we all grow parochial and blind to our own professional absurdities. And very possibly we don't often come close enough to other professions to observe and take warning from them.

Now local news: Mr. Peters, a dangerous handyman with a saw, has been making some 'improvements' to brighten his little front garden in the winter and perhaps also to keep his mind off his very tiresome mother. The new effort is a sort of doll's house, in the middle of the lawn, beside which stands a pottery gnome. On the doll's house are painted the words A GNOME AWAY FROM 'OME. You won't believe it, but it's perfectly true!

Don't you think that garden ornaments and accessories in general have sunk to a pretty low level? More than a hundred years ago, Loudon wrote in his *Encyclopaedia of Gardening* that 'mock hermits, soldiers, banditti, wooden lions and sheep in stucco', though still to be found in continental gardens, were 'too puerile for the present age'. Yet even at Chelsea, where they ought to know better, you can still see terrible concrete whimsies; and the design of wrought-iron gates, sundials and bird-baths is often shocking. I can't believe that a garden seat I saw there last year was improved by the inscription:

WHERE THE ROSE AND LILY MEET
WE ARE SITTING AT GOD'S FEET

Far better if the time and money spent on carving it had been devoted to a study of the contours of the *human* seat; it looked hideously uncomfortable.

Mr. Peters, hearing that I'm a keen gardener, has sent me a message by Ovenden telling me of a firm that's selling gnomes off cheap. I was so terrified that one or other of them might give me a few for Christmas, that I thought it wise to make my attitude to gnomes perfectly plain.

Incidentally, I'm trying to design a sundial—something monolithic and simple—and I'm finding it much more difficult than I'd expected. It's to go on the terrace, which seems to need a focal point of some kind, and I've been told of a local mason who can cut the stone for me. What shall I have for a motto? I favour something astringent, such as

It's later than you think

or Hilaire Belloc's

I am a sundial, and I make a botch
Of what is done far better by a watch.

Have you any good ideas?

Helen Parker has been to tea. She told me, without any encouragement on my part or a trace of self-pity on hers, the story of her pretty wretched life: poverty, brutal father who drank, dreary governess jobs abominably paid, at last a chance of teaching the piano at a decent school, and then the collapse of her health. She's frightfully poor, but courageous and cheerful—almost aggressively cheerful. She wears rimless glasses and has one of those 'bright' schoolmistressy voices that get on one's nerves. She knows everything that goes on in the village, and she never stops talking:

'It's so *jolly* you've come to live here; the Trotters were such *dull* people. Mind that step! it's loose. You know about Mr. Trotter, of course? The verdict was "accidental death", but one always wonders in a case like that. . . . It's fairly certain he was in financial difficulties and would have had to sell the house. Mrs. Trotter is living in a small bungalow near Maidstone and is already having trouble with the drains. The son is in Australia—and doing no good there, I'm told. . . .' And so on, *ad nauseam*.

I felt that I could report to Delia that I'd been 'perfectly sweet' to Miss Parker; but I also felt very exhausted.

November 8th

When I said that Nature (like Mr. Trotter) sometimes uses a gun, I ought really to have said a sling and a catapult. At Kew, when no one is looking, I like touching the ripe seed-pods of the touch-me-not balsam; there's a sudden sharp crack like the breaking of the mainspring of a watch, the pod is ripped open and the seeds flung into the air. The mechanism is roughly that of the mouse-trap, the tension being produced by the swelling and contraction of certain tissues.

It's just one of Nature's many ways of dispersing seed. The seeds of aquatic plants travel chiefly by water, but there are land plants whose fruits float and can cross oceans without damage—the coconut for one; asparagus seed will germinate after a whole year in salt water.

Wind carries many seeds, their flight assisted by every kind of wing, sail and parachute. The various so-called 'resurrection plants' uproot themselves bodily after flowering, roll themselves into hedgehog-like balls and bowl away across country until it starts to rain, when they expand and disperse their seeds. One of these— the rose of Jericho (*Anastatica hierochuntica*)—fascinated the crusaders and medieval pilgrims, who carried specimens of it back to Europe.

Animals (man included) transport seeds. Some cling by hook, claws, barbs, or sheer stickiness to fur, feathers and trouser-legs. Squirrels and ants remove others to their larders and often forget about them, and man-made British Railways (Western Region) have carried the Oxford ragwort over their entire network. Various seeds pass unharmed through the bodies of birds and other animals, and Kerner made elaborate experiments on the subject. That tomato seeds will pass without damage through the human body was brought home to me when I once saw a garden where sludge from the local sewage works had produced a fine crop of tomato seedlings.

But my favourites remain the slung and the catapulted. Gerard describes the squirting cucumber that 'oftentimes striketh so hard against those that touch it (especially if it chance to hit against the face) that the place smarteth long after;' and Goethe, during his visit to Italy, was woken one night by the explosion of acanthus seed-pods that he'd picked and put in an open box. The finest and noisiest performance is given by the sandbox tree (*Hura crepitans*), an Indian shrub which explosively propels its inch-long seeds a distance of up to fifty feet. This I can't hope to grow, but I'm going to try the squirting cucumber if I can get seed of it.

Three days after Helen Parker had been here, I received one of those '*any* day next week, *or* the week after' invitations to tea with her. It wasn't that I wanted to refuse, but I do think invitations ought to leave one a loop-hole. Also I have the impression that she might become rather *too* clinging. But perhaps I am quite wrong; Helen simply adores any opportunity of talking to anyone.

She lives alone in a tiny cottage—one in a row—with a garden 14 ft. by 8 ft. in front (I've measured it) and one about three times the size at the back. She tells me that, added together, they're smaller than one side of a tennis court, and I can well believe it. The Japanese say of a very small garden that it's 'as narrow as a cat's forehead'. I don't know enough about cats to see the point, but I expect you'll be able to explain; anyhow, there's no doubt that Helen's qualifies as such.

I must admit that she's been absolutely brilliant with her 'gardens' (she insists upon the plural). The back garden, which is walled, has a terrace, a lawn, a blue-tiled fountain with a squirt the size of a fountain-pen filler, a herbaceous border, and a shrubbery. And by means of brightly-painted tubs and suspended flower-pots, red-lacquered bamboo canes and chicken-wire, and so on, she manages, as the Spaniards do in their *patios*, to give the impression of a blaze of colour all the year round.

She grows the plants she likes, however unfashionable or unwisely rampageous. I noticed, for example, that she had *Campanula rapunculoides*, and suggested that it was rash to introduce it into a small garden. But of course she was perfectly right in saying that it wasn't: in such a confined space she can watch its growth inch by inch, and keep it under perfect control.

I admired an immensely healthy camellia, full of buds. 'Doesn't it look jolly,' she said. 'I upset a whole bottle of Growquick on it by mistake. I think I must have given it about a hundred times the normal dose.' Now if you or I did that, the plant would be dead within a week!

She has pretty things in the house—nice bits of china and pottery, mostly broken and so picked up at junk shops for a few pence. But it must be a nightmare living in those tiny rooms, even for someone as small as she is. Her one little piece of self-indulgence is being a Fellow of the R.H.S. and going up to London three or four times a year to see their shows. She is, in fact, a thoroughly *good* person; but I still have the feeling that if given any encouragement she may become something of a bore.

Oh yes—she has another extravagance: she is perfectly reckless with pen-nibs. She says it boosts her morale to have just *one* thing in which she throws economy to the winds.

I've had a delightful visit from David. We had a long talk, and I thought he'd come on a lot since Marlborough days. Of course he's got all the glorious arrogance of youth. He said that a young Hungarian Jew named Blobwitz (?), who, it seems, is having an exhibition in Dover Street, was 'as great as, or even greater than, Michelangelo'; as I hadn't seen any of his work I was at a disadvantage, but I ventured to doubt it all the same. The same kind of nonsense about music and poetry. We argued amicably, but we had no illusions about each other: I knew he thought me an old square; he knew I thought him a young pup.

Probably flowers was the only subject upon which we more or less agreed. At all events it was pleasant to find that the words 'kitchen sink' meant, for both of us, a potential receptacle for little rock plants and small bulbs; for most of the younger generation they stand only for a particularly sordid kind of drama or painting. Then, too, plant-breeders haven't as yet succeeded in creating atonal anemones or surrealist sunflowers. We mayn't all like exactly the same flowers; we do at least have roughly the same idea of what flowers are aiming at.

David was full of his new tape-recorder. These machines seem to have become status symbols of the young, along with expensive cameras and projectors of various kinds, gramophones, television sets, transistors, sports cars and so on—and David has the lot; at his age I had a twenty-five shilling Kodak and a second-hand bicycle and considered myself lucky. Yes, I agree with you: he's become very good-looking—in a Nordic kind of way. Takes after his mother, of course. But I think she's going *too* far when she says that she grows those fearful delphiniums because he looks so well in among them. In any case, he's never at home in June.

I'm so very glad to hear that you're being well looked after and that you're not getting much pain now. Thank God for modern drugs!—it must have been terrible being ill a hundred years ago. Interflora should be depositing some flowers on you soon; I'm afraid they'll be very 'shoppy' and you'll probably hate them, but it's the best I can do at the moment. I'll send you some stylosas as soon as they start flowering; there are quantities of them, planted of course by Trotter's predecessor but thriving, as they always seem to, on total neglect.

Delia is having a sherry party for me to meet some more of the locals, and I'll report in due course. To judge from those I've met so far, Dewbury really is a most *incredible* backwater! Two World Wars and a hundred international crises seem to have left it quite untouched, though it did get a few bombs in 1940. Except for Colonel Stringer, nobody seems to worry about Russia or China or South Africa or whatever the current scare or problem is. London might be five hundred miles away, and but for the few 'commuters', nobody goes there if it can possibly be avoided; for some of the villagers it's quite an event to go to Dorking. I said something the other day about 'Miss Mitford's last book', only to find that my hearer assumed I meant *Mary* Mitford—who has, after all, been dead a hundred years, but who would still be very much at home in Dewbury. How angry—or how amused?—Nancy would be!

Which reminds me—have you read the Pompadour book? If not, I'll send it you.

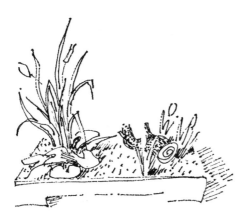

November 14th

I'm glad my stylosas arrived in good condition: the first batch. Yes—I too shall go on calling them that, and my *Chaenomeles speciosa* a japonica. These can now be considered English names.

There isn't much fresh that one can say about this miserable business of plant names. How I agree with Kit Smart: 'the right names of flowers are yet in heaven; God make gardners better nomenclators,' and with Southey, who wrote: 'As for the scientific names of Plants, if Apollo had not lost all power he would have elongated the ears of Tournefort and Linnaeus, and all their followers, as deservedly as he did those of Midas.' An international Committee meets regularly to chop and change 'nomenclatures', and the unfortunate gardener must grin and bear their decisions. The

Committee works to rules that are I'm sure sound
enough in theory; but they're certainly mad in practice.
Old errors, when intentional, are perpetuated: wist*e*ria,
named after Wist*a*r, must be kept because it was so spelt
when first described. The japonica has had no less than
five different names during my lifetime. Names may be
misleading, hard to pronounce, hard to spell, or all three.
I don't know what to suggest, because I haven't sufficiently studied the facts. If the 'splitters' are *sure* that
Lilium giganteum isn't really a Lilium, then I suppose it
must be removed from that genus. But *are* they sure?
Will there ever be agreement as to what constitutes a
genus? Mayn't a new 'lumper' come along and put it
back among the lilies?

Might it perhaps be possible for specific names that
have been accepted for a certain number of years, to be
retained, even if the botanists discover that priority
really belongs to another? After all, as Proust said,
'Rien n'est plus sacré qu'un ancien abus.'

One or two of the worst horrors of nomenclature
seem, however, to have been spirited away during the
last hundred years. There is mention, in the *Floricultural
Cabinet* for 1842, of *pollopostemonopetalæ* and *eleuthero-
macrostemones*, names which aren't to be found in the
R.H.S. *Dictionary*; and where, today, could one order
an *iztactopotzacuxochieliæhueyo*?

Yet for sheer absurdity the *birds* have it every time.
How about the little wren—*Troglodytes troglodytes troglodytes*? However, I mustn't go on flogging a dead *Equus
caballus*. . . .

And talking of flower names, do you know about that 'curious Gentleman', Mr. P. Belandine, and his ingenious idea for naming florists' flowers so that the purchaser would know what colour they were? It was a little dodge that he picked up on the Continent about 1730. His proposal was that the initial letters of the name, or names, should give the clue. If the flower was white flecked with crimson, then it could be called 'William the Conqueror' or 'Wonder of Constantinople'—the principal colour being given first. And he drew up a list of colours in which ambiguity was avoided: for example, 'S' (sable) stood for black, leaving 'B' for blue.

There was the problem of what to do about varieties already named in a way that did not conform to the Belandine rules. For instance, the 'Princess Amelia' carnation was, unfortunately, a white flower with violet markings. Belandine renamed it 'Princess Amelia, Worthy Virgin'! A neat idea—but it never caught on in England.

You say how surprising it is that the stylosa, which comes from Algeria (and also, in fact, from the Greek end of the Mediterranean), not only survives but even flourishes in England. I suppose it's a plant of the mountains, and perhaps you didn't know that 400 French soldiers were frozen to death in the Algerian uplands during the French conquest of the country. Algeria, even when there isn't a war on, is not quite the sub-tropical paradise that many people imagine. Incidentally *Iris histrioides*, which grows in Asia Minor in the same latitude as Naples, stands up to rough weather far better than stylosa.

Helen has been telling me about Mrs. Wycherley's talk to the W.I. on Japanese flower arrangements, and she was very funny about it. Mrs. Wycherley, who lives in Reigate, has been giving this talk to W.I.s all over the neighbourhood; her husband was a diplomat and *en poste* in Tokyo in the twenties.

It seems that Mrs. Wycherley was in a way quite absurd, yet at the same time a triumphant success; it never really became clear whether she was a lunatic, an inspired evangelist, or a very clever music-hall comedienne. She arrived (in Japanese dress) with a car-load of bamboo containers, bull-rushes, chrysanthemums, lumps of rocks and pieces of driftwood, which she revealed like a conjurer producing a rabbit out of a hat. Then she said (with a slightly Japanese accent), 'We will now sit in silence for five minutes, to establish a relaxed and carefree mood.' Everyone sat motionless, with deadpan expressions, for what seemed like an hour to Helen, who, she told me, would hardly have been surprised if tongues of fire had descended and she had found herself talking broad Japanese to Mrs. Wishart.

At last Mrs. Wycherley slowly emerged from her trance and announced that she followed the traditions of the Bisho School of floral arrangement. 'Our great founder, Bishoken Dogaku, who had a private income of 50,000 koku a year, said, "Always smile slightly when you touch a flower". Ladies, I beg you to do so too.' Then Mrs. Wishart was selected to come on to the platform, where she was rushed into a spare kimono and made to kneel, touch a chrysanthemum and smile slightly. I can't tell you all, but you can imagine the rest—Mrs. Wycherley gesturing the basic signs of heaven, earth and man, and all the ladies doing it in chorus, and so on: sheer *opera buffa*. Delia was also present, and I'm looking forward to hearing her account.

The evening closed with a competition, judged by popular vote, for the best new names for four familiar flowers:—celandines, daisies, convolvuluses and cow parsley. Delia's entries, said Helen, were 'yellow perils', 'shirt buttons', 'twisters' and 'old lace'. The winner was Mrs. Muchrather, with 'sunny Jims', 'faerie fancies', 'dainty dishes' and 'doilies'. I'm told that the village is now full of women carrying home lumps of rock and bits of old tree-trunks—and smiling slightly.

Isn't it strange—I'm suddenly, but only momentarily, rather *bored* with flowers! Ruskin says somewhere that this can happen to all but the very simple-minded, to whom flowers are a solace always. I shall doubtless recover with the opening of the first Roman hyacinth, but don't be surprised if my next letter is less flowerful than usual.

P.S. On looking up the stylosa, I find that in Algeria it grows 'around Algiers almost down to sea level' and is *not* a plant of the mountains. It's far braver than I'd realized.

I've just noticed in the R.H.S. Dictionary, 'Mac-palxochitlquahuitl—see *Cheirostemon platanoides*.'

E

November 25th

I love to think of you in your warm swimming-pool,
but it's disappointing that you still can't move your left
leg at all. However, you obviously have confidence in
your house surgeon, and *he* doesn't sound at all worried.
I'm sure it will come in time.

I'm afraid I've been neglecting you, so I'll try to
make up for it now by telling you about Delia's party. It
was tremendous fun. It's clear that she's the uncrowned
queen of the neighbourhood and adored by everyone—
except Mrs. Puttenham and Mrs. Moon.

She'd told me to arrive early so that she could prime
me about the people who were coming. I was greeted by
over-demonstrative dogs and the largest and strongest
cocktail imaginable: 'Darling! Drink it up quick: you'll
need it. And could you *bear* to open those three bottles?
Humphrey isn't back from London yet. You haven't

met Humphrey, have you? He's absolutely fascinating
—and *so* unexpected.'

One of the dogs began eating a large piece of coal on
the hearth-rug, making a fearful mess. I pointed it out
to Delia, but all she said was, 'Sweetie-pie! Isn't it funny
how dogs like coal—coal and stamps? Hither ate a five-
pound roll of threepenny stamps last week—didn't you,
Sweetie? One of the most wonderful things about dogs
is that you can tell them how much you love them without their thinking you want to sleep in their baskets.
And now I'll tell you who's coming.

'First there's General Cornish. He's an *absolute* angel
and got several V.C.s in the Boer War (I think) and was
frightfully brave when we had the bombs in 1940. Mrs.
Cornish doesn't really appreciate him. Then there's
Archdeacon de Vie: he can tell you the date of every
font in England—and probably will. And the Wadding-
tons: he's a surgeon and she works as his secretary and
is an *absolute* slave. Darling! do be *perfectly* sweet to her;
I don't think she has much fun. And there's Susanna
Tumaniantz who's Armenian and quite mad and always
loses things and it would take me a week to tell you all
about her but one day I will. The Stringers of course
you've met already. I always think he'd make the *perfect*
husband because he knows the answer to everything
and he'd be such a *tower of strength* in a crisis. Don't you
think he's *terribly* good-looking? Oh, and of course
there's the Admiral—George Downes. He wears a
monocle and has an absolutely *divine* bull-terrier and
he'll be the last to go and he'll be just a *tiny* bit unsteady.

He's an absolute *angel*. And there's Eric Leighton and poor Pamela. He knows much more about flowers than you do and he bullies his wife. *Do* be sweet to her. Isn't it odd how men are so much nicer than women?'

I was about to say that I could think of many exceptions to this rule, and that it sounded as though Mr. Leighton might well be one of them, but she cut me short. 'Anthony Hill possibly you *won't* like. He collects early English watercolours, which is always a sign of arrested development—like stamps. And have you met Oliver Puttenham? He's that *awful woman*'s youngest son and he's fifteen and he's perfectly sweet and Darling you'll *absolutely* love him. I ask him over here as often as I can, to get him away from his mother. *Promise* to see that he only has sherry. He's just left Harrow rather hurriedly, actually in the middle of the term—or whatever they call it there; all the Puttenhams have been at Harrow since the time of Charlemagne. His mother says she took him away because the food was bad . . . but do you *really* think . . . in the *middle* of the term. . . .? And then . . .'

But the catalogue was cut short by the arrival of the Cornishes. Delia went to the door, and I heard their rather gushing apologies for being over-punctual. Then, before the Cornishes had come into the room, a car shot past the drawing-room window and drew up with a screech of brakes. I noticed that one of the front mudguards was badly buckled, and heard a voice say, 'It's nothing. I only hit a tree.' It was Humphrey Lovell.

I quite realize that Delia's conversation, when transferred to paper, may seem rather gushing, and her 'Darling' appallingly dated. But it isn't so in the least—I promise you. Spoken in a languid or a fruity voice the very same words might sound affected or even rather silly; but her voice is like a very dry champagne, her words brittle—it's no use, I can't explain. You must wait until you can hear it for yourself. Which reminds me that I've probably got a surprise for you, but I'm going to keep it to myself for the moment because it isn't quite fixed yet.

To return to the party. There were about twenty people in all, and I didn't get some of them properly sorted out. The ones who principally registered were the Admiral, Miss Tumaniantz, Eric Leighton and Oliver Puttenham. In any case they'll be enough for you to go on with.

The Admiral is clearly a glorious character, and more like an admiral than any I've ever met before. I suppose he's in his late sixties, very weather-beaten, very bluff and not at all 'silent Navy'. He'd be splendid in 'Pinafore'. He can't pronounce his 'r's'. From his conversation you'd imagine that there wasn't a sea battle this century in which he hadn't played a prominent part, not an admiral with whom he wasn't on slap-bottom terms (*but wait!*); he said his hobby was 'felling twees', and offered his services at Orchards.

Miss Tumaniantz is also turned sixty, I should guess: enormous, black, Jewish-looking, with nine-tenths of a moustache. She made a dead set at me, said she'd heard

I was so brilliant and well-informed, and what did I think about the group of young Armenian sculptors who were taking Paris by storm? '*You* must tell *me*,' I said (I'd never heard of them). So she did—at great length. It seems that they work entirely with barbed wire. They're desperately poor and have everything in common—clothes, beds, barbed wire cutters even; but especially beds. Miss Tumaniantz said she spoke frankly, as artist to artist. I would appreciate that 'genials' (as she called them: her English is patchy) couldn't be bound by conventional morality. I asked if she herself painted. She said, 'No—but I write *important* poetry. I will show it you one day'. 'Do you write in English?' 'No—but I have *traductions*.'

Eric Leighton I didn't take to at all. I thought of *snakes*. 'You must come and see my garden one day, if it would *amuse* you,' he said in an affected voice. 'I've one or two *trifles* that might interest you. I'm surprised you bought Orchards if you're a gardener; you can't grow anything *interesting* on that soil. I'll let you have some *bits and pieces* later on, if you like. What do you *specialise* in?'

Oliver Puttenham and I got on excellently. He likes gardening, but isn't allowed to do any at home. 'Mother says there's no point in paying gardeners huge wages and then doing their work for them. Orchards was in a fearful mess when the Trotters were there; can I come and help you tidy it up? Actually I'm rather at a loose end at the moment.' I said I'd be only too pleased. Oliver likes classical music, and wants to come and play my gramophone too. He's gay and ingenuous and very young for his age; I think he'd be fun to have about the place. I wonder what the trouble was at Harrow.

Oh—there was one very funny moment. In a sudden pause in the general conversation Helen Parker was heard to announce, in a slightly pompous and very penetrating voice, 'I have an aunt in Cambridge on rather heavy soil. . . .' The silence embarrassed her and she broke off abruptly. Everyone laughed, and then Archdeacon de Vie said, 'My dear lady! If that's a verse from "The Church's one foundation" it's one I don't know.' Delia said, 'No, Darling; "From Greenland's icy mountains".'

In fact there were *two* funny moments, but nobody except me heard poor Mrs. Stringer say to Eric Leighton that she simply *adored* Monteverdi's operas— 'especially *Aida*'! Leighton said 'Indeed!' very coldly, and turned away in search of higher-brow conversation.

The Admiral left last and lurching as predicted, taking Miss Tumaniantz's umbrella and spectacles-case with him since he was passing her door; and I couldn't help feeling that Oliver also had drunk quite enough. Delia said, 'Darling, now I'm going to mix you a *proper* drink—you haven't had anything—*and* you're staying to supper because it's Humphrey's birthday and we're opening a bottle of rather special hock. Isn't the Admiral an *angel*, I saw you having a long talk with him.' I agreed, and made some remark about his distinguished career. Delia said, 'It wasn't particularly distinguished—Burma Forestry. . . . Darling, you didn't

really think he was an admiral, did you?' I said, of course
I did. Why shouldn't I? He gave me a most graphic
account of the Battle of the River Plate and how—was
the whole thing simply a joke?

Delia was convulsed with mirth. 'Darling, did he
really tell you that? You didn't *really* believe him, did
you? How *terribly* funny! Everyone calls him the
Admiral because he looks so exactly like one, and he's
almost come to believe it himself. Humphrey darling,
you *must* hear this frightfully funny story. . . .'

There's lots more I'd like to tell you (and first, that
Humphrey really *is* as nice as Delia), but I'm so sleepy
that I can't write any more; and I want this to catch the
early morning post.

Ever your very affectionate godfather

Wilfrid Sharp

P.S. Before I forget, I find that what I wrote last
week about nomenclatures was not quite correct. The
Committee drew up the Rules and periodically revises
them; it doesn't decide on particular cases, except on
which generic names are to be kept. The chaos is
chiefly caused by those eager botanists who attack a
particular group of plants and 'lump' or 'split' them
until they become unrecognizable. I know they have a
difficult job; but, to put it mildly, they've got us into a
most infernal mess.

DECEMBER

December 1st

My dearest Flora,

It's an unspeakable day—the third such day running: east wind like a knife, snowing a bit too. One of the great joys of retirement is that one can just sit indoors, feet up in front of the fire, and read; as a Persian proverb says, 'The fireside is the tulip-bed of a winter day'. A bowl of Roman hyacinths and a glass with a few stylosas remind one that this horror can't go on for ever.

I fear that adequate floristic coverage was not evidenced by my last letter—as the American botanists would say, so let me commence by updating you with the motivations of my current thinking botanywise. First, I've been browsing in Batchelor and Webber's monumental *The Citrus Industry*, to try to find out about grapefruit. Curious that in a book of nearly 2,000 pages there should be only one brief and rather apologetic reference to marmalade! And it didn't tell me what I most wanted to know: when grapefruit first reached the

English market—a date which deserves to be celebrated in our annals. But of course it's an American book, and why should the Americans care? The first record of grapefruit comes from Barbados in 1750, where it was usually known as 'the forbidden fruit'. I wonder why.

Then I've been having another look at Kerner von Marilaun's *Natural History of Plants*. It's more than sixty years old now, and no doubt quite out of date. Though I can't of course understand it all, I think it's the model of what a book of that kind ought to be. Did you ever, as a child, read those books called *Marvels of the Universe*, *The Romance of Plant Life*, *Flowers and their Unbidden Guests*, and so on? I found them irresistible. I was fascinated to discover that the total length of the roots of a well-grown cucumber was 15 miles, that there were 400,000,000 microbes in a cubic inch of good soil, and that the worms at work in an acre of cultivated land would, if laid end to end, stretch from the Marble Arch to Waltham Cross. I remember reading somewhere that if all the tea drunk in England in a single day were made into a lake, it would be big enough to float a large battleship. And if all the beer . . .?

Then there were the photographs—pretty poor really, but I found them exciting enough. I remember one of a coach-and-four being driven through a tunnel cut in the bole of a Douglas fir, and another of a small black baby sitting on the leaf of a giant water-lily. Also another, very odd, of an 'ithyphallic aroid' . . .

Oh, I know!—there was plenty in those books too that I couldn't understand, but the new ones are worse.

For all their catch-penny titles, these bouncing volumes of 'popular' science, these *Microseismology for the Millions* and *Bionomics for the Billions*, are almost incomprehensible to the millions and billions who buy them trustingly and then leave them lying about, unread, on occasional tables. Don't you agree? Scientific writers *have* to use scientific jargon, which has become baby-prattle to them; but they never seem able to realize that their readers are being hopelessly left behind.

I can forgive John Evelyn his 'emuscation' (demossing), 'ablaqueation' (laying bare the roots), 'stercoration' (dunging), and so on, because these words have at least a period splendour; and in any case he appends a glossary. But today a botanist will write 'parthenocarpy' just as casually as you or I would write 'parsley'—and most of his public will think that the word has something to do with a large Greek temple and a large freshwater fish. In Dr. Turrill's *British Plant Life*, a volume in the popular 'New Naturalist' series, there are pages on end where I can't understand a single word. Even my friend Patrick Synge, a most civilized and urbane writer, expects the reader of his *Plants with Personality* to know what proteolytic enzymes are. Do *you*?

Susanna Tumaniantz has been much in evidence at Orchards. The Admiral is reported to have said of her that she's succeeded, at one time or another, in losing everything she possesses except weight and her virginity, and Delia's *bon mot* was 'old in years but Jung at heart'. Most of her relations and all her property she lost in the Turkish massacres at Mush, but a brother, who has a business in London, is rich and supports her. Poor Susanna is madly fond of cream buns and anything in trousers; she indulges unrestrainedly in the former, but so far the 'elders' have eluded her. She has a memory like a sieve, and never returns from Dorking with her full complement of glasses, bag, umbrella and purse. The village post office is always placarded with a catalogue of her more recent losses.

Though she has lived in England for forty years, Susanna has never mastered the subtleties of our language. I met her yesterday at the bus stop: 'I go to London to *Wozzeck*', she informed me. She had a basket and was looking quite awful in tight-fitting magenta jeans. 'When?' I asked; she was obviously going shopping in Dorking. 'Yesterday,' she replied. Or this:— Susanna, on the subject of a mutual acquaintance: 'He is so *ungrateful*. He feeds the hand of the dog that bites him, as you say in England.'

Now what specially interests me about Susanna is her garden. Not that there's ever much in it, I'm told—in spring she refers to it as 'really a *summer* garden', and vice versa—but I gather that she *does* grow some of the wild flowers that she remembers from her childhood days in Mush. Her brother trades with the Turks (though of course he hates them) and has managed to smuggle in various plants—tulips chiefly. It's rather alarmingly clear that Susanna has taken a fancy to me, and I think that in exchange for buns I might get tulips. I'm longing for the spring, to see what she has.

Delia tells me that the Admiral is a tremendous man

with an axe and saw. A piece of woodland went with his house when he bought it. The Admiral did some thinning (which it needed), then some more thinning (which it didn't). Next he cut down the Banksian rose on the house because it was damaging the wisteria, then the wisteria because it was darkening the rooms. He cut down the laburnums and red mays because they were suburban, some lilacs because they blocked the view, and a fine red chestnut for no reason at all. When the whole place looked as though a battle had been fought over it, he planted a lot of miscellaneous quick-growing trees. 'And he hopes,' said Delia, 'they'll be big enough to cut down before he dies. I wish you could have seen it all ten years ago when old Mrs. Mason lived there; it was a dream.'

No news from your mother, who is too busy preparing for the Silver Wedding to have time to answer letters (for example, the one I wrote ten days ago asking if I could be of any help!). She tells me that Doris has now gone, and she hasn't yet been able to replace her.

December 8th

First I must tell you about the Silver Wedding. Your mother very kindly offered to put me up for it, but I can't any longer face Kingsmead in mid-winter. What *is* the point of having central heating if you turn it off when the temperature touches 50 degrees? I now require a written guarantee of 65° in the drawing-room and 55° minimum in the bedroom before I accept any invitations between November and the end of March. 'Archie sends *warmest* love,' your mother concluded her letter; it's an old and private joke between your father and me, and means, poor old boy, that he's freezing.

But of course I went over—for the day. Your mother says she's written you a full account, so I'll only tell you things she probably won't have mentioned. To begin with, she herself looked *splendid*—really not a day over forty. As you know, I've been half in love with her for half my life, and she's as handsome today as she was when I first met her—which must be nearly thirty years ago now. But I'm worried about your father. He admits he's been 'overdoing it rather', but neither your mother nor the doctor can get him to slow down, and it would need an Act of Parliament to get your mother to turn up that heating. I've butted in too, but only to get snubbed for my pains.

How is it that you've so much taste, when both your parents (much though I love them) have none? Your mother managed to make the house look uglier than usual for the occasion—and dangerous too, as I'll tell you in a moment. She'd decided that for a Silver Wedding the decorations ought to be silver—or at least white. She'd spent a small fortune on white chrysanthemums (perfectly all right), but the trouble came over the silver. Of course she made copious use of her grey-and silver-leaved plants—all those 'nevergreens', as you call them; but she still wasn't satisfied. So, having bought a couple of tins of aluminium paint from Timothy White's and a nasal spray from Boots, she brought in rhododendron boughs from the garden and started to spray. Nothing happened: the paint was too thick. She then remembered that your father had a large bottle of hair-lotion that he never used, and the unhappy idea struck her that she might use it both to dilute the paint and at the same time produce what she called 'a springy smell'. All this was done on the evening before, and the 'floral decorations' were set up before the aluminium paint— which now sprayed beautifully—was dry. David (who told me all this) helped her; he says they both got smothered in silver.

In the morning the whole house reeked like an actress's bedroom (said your father, and your mother asked him how he knew). Windows were opened everywhere, but the fire in the drawing-room, which hadn't been lit for years, began to belch smoke and they had to be shut again. Your mother fetched bottles of Airwick, and soon there was a compound smell of smoke, hair-lotion and Airwick that was absolutely nauseating. At midday, just as the first guests were arriving, David suddenly noticed that your father's back was streaked with silver paint: the hair-lotion in it had prevented it from drying!

The guests were warned as they arrived, but by the end of the afternoon almost everyone had been more or less silvered. They took it in good part—all except Mrs. Dagleish. She'd just been telling a Mrs. Leggett, with a certain relish, that her dress was ruined, and Mrs. Leggett couldn't resist saying, 'Do you know what your hair looks like—*at the back*?' However, on the whole it was a great success. But I'd be amused to know how much of all this your mother mentioned in her letter to you.

Turning now to the subject I wrote about last week: another thing that these scientific writers imagine is that if they scatter here and there a modish phrase or two, a whimsical little jest, a simile from the greater world that exists outside their drab laboratories, or a placebo such as 'and here our little friends the bacteria enter the story. . . .'—then all will be cosy and plain. Last year a botanist lent me a book which he said I'd enjoy—W. O. James's *Background to Gardening*. Bits of it I did—but bits of it I didn't. It must be meant to be 'popular', because it's got that old *Punch* joke about mummified cats and 'Egyptian fur-tiliser' and other such whimsies in it. But what about this? I made a copy of it and can't resist sending it you:

> The elements . . . then become positively charged cations and negatively charged anions respectively and can only exist in loose association with ions of

charge opposite to their own. In the soil solution there are cations of potassium (K^+), calcium (Ca^{2-}) and other metals balanced by chloride (Cl^-), sulphate ($SO_4{}^{2-}$), phosphate ($H_2PO_4{}^-$) and other anions. The loose electrovalent links between particular pairs of ions are not binding and irrevocable; they might be compared with those between ordinary engaged couples or married film stars.

That little joke at the end, like the Egyptian fur-tiliser, is there to show you that Professor James, for all his great learning, is really quite human after all. But does it take you a fraction of an inch nearer understanding what it's all about? We've been told that these electrovalent links—whatever they are—are 'loose', 'not binding' and not 'irrevocable'; couldn't you have thought up that bit about the matrimonial life of film stars for yourself? Wouldn't you far rather have been told what an anion and a cation were? They appear to be Greek words meaning 'going up' and 'going down'. Some kind of a lift, perhaps.

I know what Professor James would say: that they're both to be found in the *Concise Oxford Dictionary*. Perfectly true; but does that help? Of course not—because *another* scientist has written the definitions, and he uses several more words that you and I don't understand! One could go on like that for ever. . . .

Well—that's enough of a lecture for one day. And anyhow, I want to look at Percy Thrower on the TV. I love to watch him being ushered in—intent on his pot

F

of azaleas, and half-obliterated by captions—to the strains of that happy little tune. Then the coat so carefully removed and hung upon the door of the utterly bogus greenhouse, the sleeves rolled up for business, the discreet disclosure of the guest-star (international expert on rock plants from Edinburgh, perhaps), the cosy duologue, and finally the musical exit among more captions and azaleas. How *well* he does it! Such timing, such assurance! But, personally, I could do with fewer Brussels sprouts.

Later. Your aunt says that you've fallen out with the house surgeon. I'm very sorry; she seems to think so highly of him. Incidentally, she's kindly offered to give me, for my sundial, a gnomon that she's found in an antique shop. I had to tell her that if it's one that's been made for Edinburgh it will be quite useless in southern England, and I could see from her reply that she considers me ungrateful and unreasonably fussy. Her letter ends, 'and anyhow you've a perfectly good watch.' Perhaps she's right: I don't suppose I'll often use it to tell the time. And yet I'd rather have the correct thing.

P.S. I noticed the other day that Ovenden, who has been keeping a record of the minimum temperatures in the greenhouse, spells Fahrenheit 'Farrenheight'; this no doubt accounts for his saying that he has no intention of abandoning the Fahrenheit scale for 'Centigrade or any other German nonsense'.

December 15th

Well—here is my surprise. Delia has to go to Scotland on Wednesday for a week or ten days, and she's going to look you up! After the great *réclame* I've made I hope you won't be disappointed. No—you *couldn't* be. It will probably be Thursday or Friday, but she'll ring up the Hospital first. I can hardly wait to hear what you think of her.

The weather is suddenly warm, and I've been hard at work planting old roses. I suppose I've got a selfish nature, because I've never felt much urge to weed other people's gardens (have *you?*). Yet I've had the Admiral cutting down a dead oak for me (and trying to cut down everything living in sight), and both Susanna and Oliver in constant attendance. If Evelyn is right in maintaining that '*Gentlewomen* may do themselves much good by kneeling upon a Cushion, and *weeding*'—then Susanna should now be in splendid fettle. Thanks to them all, and with Ovenden coming three days a week, I've got the worst of the jungle clear before the real winter is upon us. The paved walk is now visible again, the borders dug, the yews clipped. Tubs for the terrace have been bought, painted, filled with soil, and planted for the time being with wallflowers (labelled WARFLOWERS in Dorking market where I bought them).

While Oliver was helping me to cut back some cherry-laurels I told him the history of the tree, which I'd just been reading up. (You know—inside almost every student is a teacher trying to get out!) The cherry-laurel first reached western Europe when the Imperial Ambassador at Constantinople, David Ungnad, sent a plant to the botanist Clusius in Flanders. This arrived in a battered and almost moribund condition and had to be nursed through an exceptionally severe winter; but in the spring Clusius succeeded in striking cuttings. A Mr. Cole first grew the cherry-laurel in England in the early part of the seventeenth century, treating it as very delicate and keeping it covered with a blanket during the winter. Then it was discovered, not only that it was pretty hardy, but also that it was extremely poisonous: Erasmus Darwin saw a large pointer dog die in a few minutes after swallowing two spoonfuls of laurel-water, and two Dublin girls were killed by eating its leaves in mistake for bay-leaves. But the laurel's greatest moment of publicity came when, in the eighteenth century, a real baronet—Sir Theophilus Boughton—was poisoned by his brother with a brew of its leaves. There was a celebrated trial and the murderer was hanged. Oliver appeared deeply interested and insisted upon taking two or three leaves home 'to study'; I hope they weren't intended for Mrs. Puttenham's supper!

I'd never have believed that Susanna, with all that weight to carry round, would have been so energetic, but she has performed miracles. She handles 'well-rotted' manure as eagerly as if it were strawberry jam (have you, incidentally, ever heard of a use for '*ill*-rotted' manure?). In return for her labours I submit to many languorous looks which have not escaped Oliver's notice. 'You'd better watch out,' he said to me; 'she's after you.' I pooh-poohed the idea, but I can't help feeling a bit apprehensive. I thought you'd be amused to hear of my latest conquest!

As for Oliver—he's very great fun, and entertains me with his inconsequent chatter and listens to gramophone records after we've had tea. 'I expect you'd like to know why I left Harrow so suddenly,' he said yesterday. 'Not particularly,' I answered, and then regretted it; because of course he shut up at once. I admit I *am* rather curious to know why. He said it was a pity that there weren't any pretty girls in the village. 'What about Daphne Usher?' I asked. (Daphne is the daughter of the Rector, who is coaching Oliver in Latin and French in the mornings; she looks like an ITV advertisement for toothpaste.) But poor Daphne was dismissed as quite impossible and '*far* too old'. I suppose she might be nineteen.

I asked him about his mother, whom I still haven't met. 'You won't like her,' he said. 'She isn't very popular round here. Delia hates her.' 'Why, has she said so?' 'No—but I can *tell*.' Poor child! I feel sorry for him. His two brothers are a good deal older than he is and work in London, and he's obviously very lonely.

Yes—you are perfectly right about *Scilla peruviana*; in spite of its name it's a Mediterranean plant, and its only connection with Peru is that that was the name of the ship which brought it to England. There's no end to absurdities of this kind. The African and French marigolds come from Mexico, the Italian jasmine from the Far East, English and Dutch irises from the Pyrenees, the French bean from South America, the Guernsey lily from South Africa. . . . Haven't you *yet* got used to the botanists' funny little ways? The 'Jerusalem' of the Jerusalem artichoke, a North American plant, is a corruption of the Italian word *girasole* (sunflower), and the 'Jordan' almond is the 'jardyne' ('garden') almond —so one can't blame *them* on the botanists!

Do drop me a line about Delia when you've seen her.

P.S. Futile conversation in a very smart flower shop in Dorking this morning, while trying to buy an outrageously expensive pot of hyacinths to bring on at home and then take to Delia for Christmas:

'Why are they so dear?'

'It's a named variety, Sir.'

'What's it called?'

'Oh, we don't know its name.'

December 23rd

Here's a happy Christmas to you—or as happy a one as you can have under the circumstances, and may you this time next year be well again and at home with your family. It's splendid that you're beginning to move the left leg a bit at last.

Your letter and Delia's arrived by the same post and I felt like that donkey between two bundles of hay—quite unable to decide which to eat first. I won't tell you all she said about you, because it might make you conceited. And you, I gather, were equally charmed. I'm delighted. I can just imagine her entry, half hidden by chrysanthemums and boxes of chocolate. I'm only surprised that she didn't succeed in getting the dogs in too, but I suppose matrons are impervious to charm. She'll be back soon and I'll no doubt get a full account of you.

I'm glad you too can say that you can't remember a
time when you didn't love flowers. I've clear recollec-
tions (and a photograph) of you, lupin-tall, watering
your garden at Kingsmead. As a child I lived in what
was then a small semi-rural parish less than ten miles
from Charing Cross; I hardly recognize it today, with
its ten thousand inhabitants, its Tudor Estate, its Bor-
stal Institute, its scream of traffic across the Common.
From the Vicarage gate I could then toddle forth and,
without fear of sports cars or abduction, cross the road
alone and pick harebells and violets (white ones even)
on the Common. What happy times they were!

I had my own pocket-handkerchief bit of garden
where I grew an odd handful of plants chosen chiefly
for the splendour of their names. I grew *Hyacinthus can-
dicans* which has since become galtonia and under that
disguise would hardly have excited me. I grew eschscholtzia which, like the editors of the R.H.S.'s four-
volume *Dictionary of Gardening*, I couldn't decide how
to spell. I think I also grew salpiglossis: I can't remember the rest.

But what I *do* remember, most clearly, is the day
when Queen Mary, then Princess of Wales, came to
tea, and how I took her to see my garden. I can remember every detail: the great and gracious lady, stiff as a
ramrod, prodding recklessly at my precious little plants
with the point of her parasol, which had a parrot's head
for handle. Then she asked if she might have a button-
hole.

I wasn't at all pleased, for the removal of even a single

flower would leave a distinct gap. 'Only,' I said, 'if you *pwomise* to put it in water when you get home': I thought that might discourage her. But it didn't; it merely seemed to cause consternation to my parents, who were of an age to know that princesses mustn't be ordered about. I was told to pick a flower immediately; with much reluctance I did, and gloomily watched its installation upon that memorable bosom.

I see it all, I really do, as clearly as if it had happened yesterday. But, wishing to be quite sure of my facts, I asked my mother. Yes, everything was exactly true—but for one small detail: it was *not* the Princess of Wales; it was a Miss Heathcote. What tricks the memory plays us! Maybe it's all linked up with those 'royal' dreams in which I find myself dining at Buckingham Palace, knee-deep in kings and queens and being the very life and soul of the party.

I'm having such a time with Susanna. She lent me her vilely-typed bundle of collected verse and asked for my candid opinion. It wasn't easy. 'Bosh' would have been the simple and honest answer, but for three reasons it was an impossible one. First, it would have been rude. Second, I might never get my tulips. And third, 'bosh' is a Turkish word—the only one in very common use in English—and one must never use a Turkish word to an Armenian.

Susanna's method of 'traduction' would appear to be to turn up each word in an Armenian-English dictionary and then select the longest or queerest of what she finds there, regardless of rhyme, rhythm or reason

—especially reason. (She's like the foreigner in the old story who concluded his letter to an English friend, 'May God pickle you!') Words such as 'pragmatical', 'sophomoric', and 'vespertine' abound. To judge by the quite ordinary English words that she doesn't know, it seems safe to assume that she can't understand any of the above. So when she came I tested her. 'What exactly do you mean by a "sterterous" flower?' I asked. She hesitated: 'It's a dark word.' 'But hasn't it rather to do with *sound*?' 'Yes, a *dark* sound;' she wouldn't commit herself further. I suppose snoring *is* a dark sound, and certainly flowers 'sleep'. 'Now snores the crimson petal, now the white'?

Her 'Spring in Mush' opens with the improbable line, 'Luteous tulips disseminate the shrubbery and calcareous rockery', and continues for a while in much the same vein; but in the middle of it there suddenly occurs the phrase 'beaten to a frazzle'. I have an awful feeling that David, if he came upon 'Spring in Mush' in an advanced literary weekly, might mistake it for poetry.

My spies tell me that champagne would be good for you, so I'm sending you a dozen half-bottles. Why don't you open one with Mr. McGrath and patch up your quarrel with him? It's a great mistake to be on bad terms with one's surgeon.

Ever your very affectionate godfather

Wilfrid Sharp

JANUARY

My dearest Flora,

Eric Leighton showed me round his garden yesterday. I don't much care being shown round other people's gardens in January: my eyes of faith are dimmer than they used to be.

Eric is a 'plantsman', immensely keen, immensely knowledgeable—and oh so immensely exhausting! Do you know this poem? It's Eric to the life:

> He loved peculiar plants and rare,
> For *any* plant he did not care
> That he had seen before:
> Primroses by the river's brim
> Dicotyledons were to him,
> And they were nothing more.

A plantsman's idea of a garden is entirely different from a horticulturist's or a flower-lover's, isn't it? He wants to grow what he can't, and preferably where it won't. Eric must have plants that are uncommon and

difficult; he's not in the least put off by the fact that
they mayn't really be worth growing. He collects them
as a man collects stamps, and what he really enjoys is
pitting his skill against Nature. If a plant is blue, Eric
won't rest until he's got hold of the rare albino form
('You won't find it anywhere in this country except at
Kew'). If it's large, he wants it small; if small, then of
course he must have it enormous. He has a horror of all
that flowers freely, and his favourite word for such
things as aubrieta is 'cats'-meat'. His ideal garden—his
own garden—is one that, even in high summer, is full of
labels, and sheets of glass suspended above almost invisible plants. You remember how the crowds flocked
to the National Gallery to gape at the gap where the
stolen Goya had been? Well, Eric stares like that—and
makes certain that *you* stare too—at the spot where the
label says there's going to be a *very special lily*.

Plantsmen have another tiresome habit. Like people
who are always talking about 'George' and 'Harry' and
expect you to know whom they mean, Eric never uses a
generic name if he can possibly help it. His plants are
all just *heterophylla* or *fragrans* or *Farreri*, and you have
to guess the rest. But Eric's great virtue is his generosity.
He'll promise you, for the autumn, a rhizome of this, a
rootling of that. And what's more, I'm told (by Helen)
that when the time comes he'll bring them round to
you, all neatly labelled and wrapped in polythene and
whether you want them or not. And he *never* forgets!

Helen also told me that Eric is a Jew of Portuguese
extraction. He does look a bit Jewish, and rather dark—

but I don't know. He certainly has Jewish shrewdness and thoroughness. It would be very difficult to swindle him. If the plants he orders arrive even very slightly damaged, or if he doesn't like the look of them for any reason, he sends them straight back with what he calls a 'firm' (and what we'd no doubt call a 'rude') letter demanding replacement.

Eric's house is ugly Victorian and far too large (he's married, but there are no children); he only bought the place because it had a well-established garden with good trees. The walls of his drawing-room are covered with his painstaking but very amateur watercolours of flowers. He has no taste; his garden is excellently planned—because it was laid out by his predecessor. But it lies in a hollow, and he says he was a fool ever to have come there because it's a frost pocket. However, the soil is good, and lime-free (which he wants); there's a little stream which he uses cleverly; and he's recently bought a small stretch of wooded hillside. It's very remote—rather *too* remote for my taste, and he's more than once been cut off for several days in winter.

That hillside, by the way, he's planted with rhododendrons, magnolias, camellias and heaths. (Somebody once said of Eric that his face had 'grown lined in the service of the rarer ericaceae'!) I know I'm a heretic, but I don't really care for rhododendrons in among English oaks and beeches. Actually I don't much like them anywhere—except the common *ponticum*: and that is utter blasphemy! I wish Eric had left it all alone—with the foxgloves, bluebells and primroses that he's so proud of having exterminated. Who was it who said that the rhododendron had become 'England's worst weed'?

Susanna has taken to dropping little letters in on me when she knows I'm out. They ask whether I can lend her any Kafka, any Kierkegaard, a pair of shears 'for one hour only', a piece of white chalk, and so on. She doesn't really want any of them; she just wants an excuse to write to me. And I notice with dismay that she has now progressed from 'Dear Wilfrid' to 'Wilfrid dear'—a well-known danger-sign. If I don't answer or act immediately on my return (which she can observe from her sitting-room window), she rings up to ask whether Mrs. Benham has given me her letter. I gather that Mrs. Benham is pretty brusque with her, which is all to the good.

Mrs. Benham is proving herself the treasure that I hoped for. Of course she has her 'little ways', some of which are mildly irritating. She's very possessive—I heard her at the back door telling the greengrocer that '*my* gentleman' didn't like oranges—and Delia is almost the only one of my women friends who gets a welcome. I find that Delia nearly always brings some little gift or other with her—a box of chocolates, a few chrysanthemums ('They're for the kitchen, Mrs. Benham. You're *not* to put them in Mr. Sharp's study—they're wasted on him').

Perhaps the most irritating of all is Mrs. Benham's almost pathological horror of wasps, flies, ants, spiders, bats and so on. I hear a scream from the kitchen and rush in, thinking that she must have fallen or scalded herself, and what do I find? Mrs. Benham crouching in one corner, a large spider crouching in the other, and her spaniel in the middle of the room, staring pityingly at her as if to say what I long to say but daren't: 'Don't be such a complete ass!' But all this is a small price to pay for absolute integrity and real kindness and goodness.

January 10th

I've been thinking about the forcing of flowers. There are two articles on the subject in the R.H.S. Dictionary, but naturally they only deal with the practical side. I'd like to know when it all started. I know the Romans used artificial heat to get roses and lilies to flower in winter, and that they grew their best grapes in forcing-houses with windows made of mica. But I was really thinking of this country, and when forcing was carried out on any scale. For how long, for example, do you imagine florists have had daffodils, hyacinths and tulips in full flower for sale at Christmas?

I suppose that in remote villages there are still people who see their first daffodil in March and their first hyacinth in April. But for most of us the excitement of the coming of spring is as thoroughly ruined by forced and air-imported flowers as is a one-o'clock lunch by half-a-pound of chocolates at half-past twelve. None the less, on a day like this I would be pretty miserable without my bowls of Roman hyacinths, and I'm not sure that I can go the whole way with Biron in *Love's Labour's Lost*:

> At Christmas I no more desire a rose
> Than wish a snow in May's new-fangled mirth;
> But like of each thing that in season grows . . .

At any rate, flowers are terribly habit-forming, and if I don't desire a rose at Christmas I do desire flowers of some kind or another; in a room without flowers I feel as naked and embarrassed as if I had forgotten to put on my trousers.

By the way—talking of forcing, I expect you know the story of the epicure who gave his guests in April one small new potato each. '*Next year's* new potatoes,' he explained.

And *at last* I've met Mrs. Puttenham! She asked me to Sunday lunch. I formed the impression that she's a monstrous woman—vulgar, arrogant, ostentatiously rich (her father was a Midlands' industrialist who got a peerage from Ramsay MacDonald). Mr. Puttenham is, very sensibly, dead.

The house has been furnished, regardless of expense or taste, in what Mrs. Puttenham calls 'period style'. There are a few good pieces of inherited furniture in among a lot of blatant fakes bought by herself, and Puttenham ancestors, over-cleaned and over-varnished, peer down from the walls. I was disgusted by the way she spoke to her butler (the village Don Juan) for having forgotten the 'serviettes'; I'm told she can only keep servants by paying them ridiculously high wages.

'You *were* at Harrow, weren't you, Mr. Sharp,' she asked, 'or was it Eton?' 'No, Mrs. Puttenham, I was at Bedales.' She looked down her nose as if there was a slight smell of escaping gas, or as if she were saying to herself, 'How *good* of me to be *slumming* like this!'

Delia, who can't stand Mrs. P., had said to me, 'Darling, don't forget to look at her *feet*!' So I noticed what an unobservant male would otherwise have missed— that she wore those rather high-heeled shoes that Jewesses love so much and which make their feet like pigs' trotters. However, she's obviously *not* a Jewess: she's the buxom British barmaid type with (dyed?) blonde hair.

After lunch Oliver took me up to the greenhouses where I was glad to make the acquaintance of Chandler, the head gardener; in all, Mrs. P. has six full-time gardeners. Chandler is clearly extremely competent and knowledgeable and I took to him immediately, though I could wish that he didn't spit so much. He loves his Latin names, and when I mentioned columbines I was politely but sharply corrected to 'aquilegias'. It made me think of those lines of Crabbe:

High-sounding words our worthy gard'ner gets,
And at his club to wondering swains repeats;
He there of Rhus and Rhododendron speaks,
And Allium calls his onions and his leeks . . .

I wondered how Chandler could stand working for
Mrs. P. When her name was mentioned, he froze; but
he was obviously devoted to 'young master Oliver', and
I had the feeling that Oliver, and no doubt the high
wages, were among the chief reasons for his continuing
to serve a mistress he despised. I enjoyed watching
Chandler with Oliver: the man so ready to impart his
knowledge, the boy so eager to learn. I had no idea what
Mrs. P. intended to do with Oliver now that Harrow
had decided that it could get along without him; had I
been Mrs. P. I would unhesitatingly have made a gardener, in some form or other, of him.

Chandler had a fine show of camellias and orchids,
few of which seem to reach the house. Clearly Mrs. P.
takes no real interest in her garden or her greenhouses,
except when she is in the mood to show them off to her
guests. Chandler volunteered to come round one evening after work to advise me about shrubs to be planted
in the spring.

I'm *so* pleased that you've managed to walk a few
steps, even if the two stalwart supporters really did all
the work. At least it's a beginning.

P.S. I've just read that forced hyacinths respond
favourably (like you?) to 'stem massage'!

January 17th

I'm reading the diary of the American consul in Algiers at the time of the bombardment by the French in 1830. He was a keen gardener, and really much more concerned about the flowering of his night-blooming cereus than about the shelling. He sat up half the night to watch the first flower open and wrote an ecstatic account of it, dutifully adding an occasional entry about the damage to the town. Obviously a very nice man, but possibly not a very good consul.

The consul's vigil reminded me of Chaucer's *aubade* to the daisy, how on May Day he rose at dawn 'to be at the resurrection of this flower':

> And down on knees anon-right I me set,
> And as I could, this freshè flower I greet,
> Kneeling alway, till it unclosed was,
> Upon the smallè, softè, sweetè grass

while Zephyrus and Flora 'gently gave to the flowers, soft and tenderly, their sweetė breath . . .'. It comes from the Prologue to *The Legend of Good Women*, which has nearly a hundred lines on the daisy and all of them lovely.

I went to Kew again yesterday, and having half-an-hour to spare I looked into the Gardens. The hoar-frost was marvellous: much better than anything your mother can achieve with aluminium paint. But it was so hideously cold that I soon took refuge in Museum 2—'Economic Products derived from Monocotyledons and Cryptogams'. It really is a *horrifying* place; even the meanest Oxford Street window-dresser could effect an improvement in ten minutes. The cases are stuffed to bursting-point with vegetables and nightmare objects of vegetable origin. Gewgaws that the most magpie of Anglo-Orientals would hardly dare to bring back to the Motherland struggle for breathing-space with oddities from nearer home: a temple modelled in ivory nut, a Formosan fan, a tablet of vegetable carbolic soap, 'a pair of Parisian anti-rheumatic shoe-pads' and 'a needle-case made by Bavarian convicts'. (One longs to know more about the Miss Hipkins who presented the Kaffir snuff-spoons.) There are things in bottles that would turn a man's stomach against pickles for a fortnight. The labels are printed in the sort of fount that one associates with parish magazines; the photographs look wan and tired; an odour of putrefaction is everywhere. . . .

Unable to bear it a moment longer, I staggered out

into the freezing, flowerless world. Not even one of those 'pendant flakes of vegetating snow'—as Charlotte Smith calls snowdrops—visible anywhere. Then, suddenly, I saw a little clump of yellow crocuses! It thrilled me. Such heroism! I thought of Matthew Prior's poem about that 'venturous flower', and stepped on to the grass to take a closer look. It was—orange peel!

Now what's the moral of all this? If I hadn't been over-curious I'd have left the Gardens elated. Is all litter really as ugly as all litter-baskets? (Have you seen the I EAT LITTER monsters on Brighton beach?) Ought one to scatter confetti where the snowdrops have come up thinly? What about artificial flowers? Artificial flowers are beginning to get the florists a bit worried, I think. Now that they're durable, washable, smellable, and almost indistinguishable from the genuine article, is it surprising that they're steadily advancing into the home? (And is there any reason why they shouldn't advance into the garden too?) I read a letter on the subject in a gardening weekly recently. The writer was scandalized: 'our great national heritage of flowers', and so on. He wrote with the righteous indignation of an R.S.P.C.A. official denouncing bull-fighting or an archdeacon deploring adultery. I noticed his address; it was the M— Nurseries. Poor chap! It was the great national heritage of his pocket that was worrying him. Why shouldn't people buy artificial flowers if they want to?

Supposing the towns continue to swallow up the countryside, and the trippers to root up the wild flowers, the time must come when gardens are shrunk to the size of hearthrugs and the bluebell is as rare as the slipper orchid is now. Then we shall have to rely entirely upon artificial flowers, which by that time will no doubt be *better* than Nature's rather amateurish efforts. As Mr. Peters said, 'artificial flowers is like dentures—much better than the real thing, once you get used to 'em'. Cézanne held the same view and used them in his still-life paintings; and surely you can't go far wrong—at the moment, at any rate—if you hitch your wagon to a Post-Impressionist!

Incidentally—what a temperamental flower the cyclamen is in the house! A month or so ago I bought a couple of identical plants from the same shop at the same time, and gave them exactly the same treatment. Yet one is now magnificent, the other dead. Why should one be left and the other taken? And why is your mother, who doesn't pretend to be an expert, so successful with them? I shall get plastic ones next year.

And now it's started to snow!

P.S. Here is a bedtime thought for you—a Chinese proverb:

> If you want to be happy for a week, Take a wife.
> If you want to be happy for month, Kill a pig.
> If you want to be happy all your life, Make a garden.

I know you can't at the moment—make a garden, I mean; but at least you can be planning what you'll do when you're well again.

January 18th

You asked me, weeks ago, to tell you what roses I had planted, and I never did. So, though I only wrote to you yesterday, I'll compile a list and give you the very varied reasons for my choice. I like any excuse to think about roses on a day like this.

Alba 'Céleste'. For the contrast of the pink flowers and the cool grey-green of the leaves, and because the men of the Suffolk Regiment are supposed to have picked them as button-holes after the Battle of Minden.

François Juranville. Because I proposed to Betty in a summer-house that was smothered with it—and then tripped over its root as we came out, and fell flat!

R. Richardii. Because it's the 'Sacred Rose of Abyssinia'; you'll find its history in Graham Thomas's *The Old Shrub Roses.*

Cuisse de Nymphe Emue. *Alias* 'Great Maiden's Blush', etc. Partly for its names.

Frau Dagmar Hastrup (Hartopp?). Partly for her hips. Also several other rugosas—loved in spite of their thorns—including

Parfum de l'Hay. Bought by mistake; I meant to order Roseraie de l'Hay.

Common Blush China. Because I had it in my garden as a child.

Variegata di Bologna. For its astonishingly vivid stripes, and because I'm fond of Bologna.

R. foetida. Because I found it in Persia in great golden drifts; and in spite of its smell. Could this be the rose that 'sprang from the sweat of Mahomet'?

Tuscany. The 'Old Velvet' rose.

William Lobb. The 'Old Velvet' moss. Both these are as lovely as they sound.

Albertine. No garden complete without it.

Madame Hardy. For her green 'eye'.

Fritz Nobis. Such a lush pink.

Blue Boy. A modern H.P.; it may not be blue, but its colour is fantastic.

R. filipes 'Kiftsgate'. For its unbelievable vigour. I've put it to run up a dead pear-tree.

Magenta. For its colour, form and smell.

La Mortola. Curiously fascinating, with its downy grey-green leaves and flowers like a white clematis. I hope it will live.

New Dawn. 'Still indispensible', as the catalogues say.

Mermaid. Another 'must'—though I could wish its flowers hadn't been compared to poached eggs coming down a chute.

Cardinal de Richelieu. For its colour—what the old gardeners used to call a 'sad' purple.

Nevada. For visitors to admire.

Château de Clos Vougeot. Because it sounds like, and looks like, and has the aroma of, a very good Burgundy. (But oughtn't it to be 'Clos de Vougeot'?)

Stanwell Perpetual. For its peppery smell, chiefly.

R. cantabrigiensis. For being so early and so vigorous.

R. Paulii rosea. To sprawl.

R. Andersonii. Like a phlox-pink wild rose.

Peace. For Mrs. Benham, who has promised to plant it where it can't be seen from the house.

Albéric Barbier. For sentimental reasons which it would take too long to describe now.

Omar Khayyam. Also for sentimental reasons—from the rose on Edward Fitzgerald's grave. This was grown from the seed of the rose once (alas no longer!) on Omar Khayyam's grave at Nishapur.

Chapeau de Napoléon. For the curious frilled sepals that give it its name.

Ispahan. 'Rose d'Isfahan'. For its long display, and for associations with Fauré and Leconte de Lisle and Persia.

Kazanlik. Best smell of all, and associated with attar of roses (but see Graham Thomas, p. 156). Its flowers 'load the slow air with their damask breath'.

Gloire de Dijon. Because it was a favourite of Jonathan's.

Félicité et Perpétue. I've always wondered what the connection could be between this lovely sprawling white rambler and these two dusky African ladies who were martyred at Carthage in the third century; I now find it was named after the daughters of one of Louis Philippe's gardeners. There is a dwarf sport 'Belle de Téhéran', *Anglice* 'Little White Pet'.

Dorothy Perkins. Yes—that surprises you! I've planted her as a kind of *memento mori*; she's exactly the same age as I am, and it's important to be reminded, from time to time, how old and mildewed and *démodé* one has become.

Oh, and Penelope, Wolley Dod, Buff Beauty, *R. rubrifolia*, Mme Pierre Oger, etc., etc. I ought next summer to have what Mr. Wheatcroft calls a 'supercolossal, extravagrandiose Tournament of Roses'.

P.S. Mrs. Benham says she doesn't like the 'old' roses—she prefers the 'moribundas'.

January 26th

We've been snowed up here for nearly a week, and there were 25 degrees of frost last night; I gather it's been as bad or worse with you. My sprightly 95-year-old friend Miss Russell writes from Albury, 'it's not as bad as the Great Ice Age—but *you* are too young to remember that'. I sometimes think that if Majorca weren't so far from the London Library I'd go and live there permanently.

Do you know that terrific description of winter in Ibn Arabshah's *History of Tamerlane*? It begins:

Then Winter unloosed his raging tempests, raising over the world the tents of his swirling clouds and roaring till shoulders trembled. All the serpents for fear of that cold fled for refuge to the uttermost depths of their Hell. Fires subsided and were quenched; lakes froze; leaves were torn from trees; avalanches rolled headlong into the abyss; lions hid in their dens and gazelles sought shelter in their lair. The world fled to God the Avenger because of Winter's prodigious vehemence. The face of the earth grew pale for fear of it; the cheeks of the gardens and the graceful figures of the woods turned to dust, and all their beauty and vigour vanished; the young shoots shrivelled up and were scattered by the winds. . . .

It's magnificent stuff—pages and pages of it, and equally lovely descriptions of flowers and spring.

Goethe translated some of it in a poem in the *West-östliche Divan* called 'Der Winter und Timur'.

In the West, snow is synonymous with heartiness: with snowballing, skating, ski-ing and general jollification. I always intend to greet it with Chinese affection and respect. I can't, of course, saddle my donkey and ride out, like the poet Mêng Hao-Jan, in search of plum-blossom; but I could at least install myself in the loggia with a hot-water bottle, half-a-dozen rugs and a jug of mulled claret and drink to the whirling flakes. In fact, however, I've only once set foot outside my front door, and then it was merely to fight my way to the village store to buy cough-mixture. Indeed, I can't help the feeling that the beauties of snow are rather over-rated: one always expects it to look like a very good Monet; actually it turns out to be a rather bad Vla-minck.

But I haven't been lonely. Oliver has been round a couple of times and we played a Mahler symphony and the whole of *Der Rosenkavalier* (which he didn't know, and liked enormously); I find that in general our tastes coincide: we're both temporarily rather tired of Mozart, whom the B.B.C. has recently 'discovered' and there-fore plugs mercilessly. And another thing: he's inter-ested in the music and in the way it's performed, not merely—as are so many of the young—in Hi-Fi. But it's odd that two years at Harrow haven't taught him better manners. I don't think I'm particularly 'stuffy', but once or twice I've found him downright rude. For example, the other day he took off, in the middle and because *he* didn't happen to like it, a record that *I* had put on! So I made him put it on again and play it right through from beginning to end, while he sulked; and then I sent him home. However, today he apologized very handsomely.

Susanna, icicle on nose, has of course been in and out on various excuses—principally to give me the latest boring bulletin on the state of her frozen plumbing; it would take more than a blizzard to keep her away. She wants me to put out slabs of meat at the bottom of the garden for famished foxes which, she says, feel the food shortage far more than birds do; but I've not the slightest intention of feeding the Stringers' dog—which is what it would amount to. Mrs. Benham has declared more or less open war on Susanna, who, since I haven't been able to get into Dorking to buy cream buns, has fared badly. On the other hand, when Oliver comes all Mrs. Benham's maternal instincts are aroused and delicious cakes appear from nowhere.

The snow has, I'm afraid, done some damage in the garden, and a big branch of the catalpa is down. We've had nearly nine inches, but now it's beginning to thaw and already there's one burst pipe: I'll spare you the details.

Naturally I've had a nice lot of time for reading, and among other things I've been amusing myself by finding out a bit about what the books call 'giants of the vegetable world', and such-like subjects; surprisingly enough, hardly any of them seem to be American.

Most authorities appear to agree that the Australian

peppermint tree (*Eucalyptus amygdalina*) is the tallest of all trees. Nineteenth-century botanists talked of 400–500 feet; but in 1888, when a handsome prize was offered for the discovery of a specimen over 400 feet high, the biggest entered was only 326 feet. That's about forty feet lower than St. Paul's: but quite impressive all the same. I now read, however, of a giant redwood in north-west California, 'the Founders Tree', which is said to be 364 feet tall. The tallest tree in Britain would seem to be either the silver fir at Kilbride, Inveraray, or the Douglas fir at Powis Castle in Wales—both about 180 feet.

It seems to be the Spanish chestnut that wins for girth; one on Etna is said to have a *diameter* of 57 feet— almost the length of a cricket pitch. Two hundred years ago the Duke of Portland drove a carriage-and-six through a tunnel that he had had made for the purpose in the Greendale Oak at Welbeck. But for longevity the oaks are quite out of it, and the famous Dragon Tree at Orotava, in the Canary Islands, appears to be the strongest candidate; 6,000 years has been suggested for its age. Length is very easily won by the seaweeds, one found off the New Zealand coast running to upwards of 900 feet though hardly thicker than a pencil.

And one mustn't forget the giants of the equatorial mountains of East Africa. These are only *relatively* gigantic: twenty-foot groundsels with woody stems, fifty-foot heathers and thirty-foot lobelias; they are admirably described by Patrick Synge in two of his books. The odd thing is finding the babies of our gardens transformed into trees; and I believe that this 'gigantism' is still unexplained.

It's also curious, isn't it, that whereas the giant mammals have died out during the last million (or whatever it is) years, the giant vegetables have survived? There are no fossils that suggest primeval trees of more mammoth size. Yet Sir Thomas Browne will have it that the animals still win:

> That the biggest of Vegetables exceedeth the biggest of Animals, in full bulk, and all dimensions, admits exception in the Whale, which in length and above ground measure, will also contend with tall Oakes.

I also came across another thing that amused me. I suppose that, given a dozen chimney-pots, a seven-foot garden wall, a reasonable expectation of life, and a 'conker', I could do what Colonel Greenwood did a hundred years ago. The Colonel planted a horse-chestnut in a flower-pot and covered the top of the pot with wire netting; then he suspended it upside-down and watered it from *above*. The chestnut, quite unsuspecting, put out its main root downwards; this reached the air—and died. But the branch-roots, not having this innate urge to grow downwards, ascended in search of moisture and flourished. The flower-pot was exchanged for a chimney-pot; a second was added, then a third, until finally the tower of pots was seven feet high. The Colonel now brought the root over the top of a wall into another similar column of earth, thus letting it for the first time turn downwards. 'When at last this much abused organ reached the ground, the colonel removed both the artificial columns; and the plant, with a naked, arching foot, fourteen feet in length, was left to its own resources.'

I do wish that the account, which I found in Hutchinson's *Popular Botany*, made things clearer, or at least that the reference to the original source—given as *Athenaeum*, 1864—were correct. Do you suppose that the tree grew and put out branches *downwards*? I can't visualize it all. Anyhow, you at least have twenty years ahead of you—which is the time it took Colonel Greenwood; why don't you try?

Ever your very affectionate godfather

Wilfrid Sharp

P.S. Delia tells me that there's a firm in Camberley which will call once a week and change and arrange artificial flowers in the home. It also sells plastic driftwood: their leaflet says that it comes 'in small segments which you push together, rather on the poppet bead principle'.

FEBRUARY

February 4th

My dearest Flora,

  The Rector, a man named Usher, asked me to dinner last night. He is a widower, late fifties, and his very pretty daughter keeps house for him. There was no one else there.

  Usher is one of a dying race—the cultivated country parson of good family. He has private means and no ambition beyond that of leading an agreeable rural life among his books, his flowers and his dogs. He performs his parochial duties conscientiously but without enthusiasm. He visits the sick regularly; but I have the impression that while he is saying exactly what they want to hear, he will actually be wondering whether it's still too early to plant out the ipomoeas.

  He hasn't moved with the times, and he hasn't the slightest desire to do so. You couldn't conceive of him Lifting up our Hearts at 7.50 a.m., installing TV in the church, or jazzing up the services. He refuses to allow the Girl Guides to process up the aisle to deposit home-spun banners round the altar; he won't run three-legged races with the choristers at the annual choir treat. His sermons are long, scholarly, and far above the heads of most of his very small congregation. Much of this information comes from Helen, who worships him and would, I've been told, much like to become the second Mrs. Usher (so my fears were groundless!).

I've been reading lately about animals and vegetables. Didn't you think that you could tell a vegetable from an animal? I certainly did. The Oxford Dictionary defines a plant as 'a living organism . . . having neither power of locomotion nor special organs of sensation or digestion'. Trevisa, translating Bartholomaeus Anglicus in 1498, says the same thing more prettily: 'Trees meve [move] not wylfully fro place to place as beestes doo: nother chaunge appetitte and lykynge, nother felyth sorowe, . . .' So the lion is an animal; the lily is a vegetable. The lily doesn't roar after its prey or move overnight into the rose-bed. But it seems that there are borderline cases which break all the rules.

I don't of course mean such fabulous freaks as the notorious 'vegetable lamb', or the goose-bearing barnacle-tree which that old liar Gerard swears he himself saw on an island off the Lancashire coast. But there are certain small aquatic vegetables that at a particular stage in their lives behave like animals. There's the Vaucheria, a little ovoid object that propels itself by lashing the water with small hairs, but which finally settles down to a vegetable existence. There is Volvox, which even Linnaeus mistook for an animal. There are the Sphaerellae . . .

As for sensation and digestion—aren't there all the insectivorous and carnivorous plants, and those mimosas that close their leaves at a touch? It would seem that the O.E.D.'s definition doesn't work. I must look it all up.

I wondered too about the minerals. Coal is 'a mineral of carbonized vegetable matter'. When does the transition from vegetable to mineral take place? What about fossils? I wish there were someone to give me the answers.

Even insects seem to get thoroughly muddled about animal and vegetable, and a Swedish botanist watched a small wasp strenuously attempting to seduce a fly orchid. (You know that insects are very short-sighted.) Then there is protective mimicry: insects like sticks and leaves, plants like stones, seeds and fruit like bugs and beetles. There's a story by Maupassant of a man who deserted his mistress for an orchid. And how many of the millions who listen to what is generally known as 'Handel's Celebrated Largo' realize that the words of it deal with Xerxes' passion for a plane tree that he came across in Lycia when he was invading Greece with his Ten Thousand? The story is so curious that I thought you might like to read John Evelyn's account, which is based on Herodotus and Aelian. Xerxes, says Evelyn, became so infatuated with this tree that,

> spoiling both himself, his concubines, and great persons of all their jewels, he covered it with gold, gems, necklaces, scarfs, bracelets, and infinite riches. In sum, he was so enamoured of it, that, for some days,

neither the concernment of his expedition, nor interest of honour, nor the necessary motion of his portentous army, could persuade him from it. He styled
it his mistress, his minion, his goddess; and, when he
was forced to part from it, he caused a figure of it to
be stamped on a medal of gold, which he continually
wore about him.

This kind of intimacy between man and plant is
commoner in the further East (some day I'll write more
about this), so I was pleased to learn that a Mrs.
Hughes-Gibb, who made a prolonged study of the behaviour of bean-leaves, found that after months of 'daily
communion' with beans she became 'warmly attached'
to some, whereas others proved to be 'dull, slow-
natured, and even apparently sulky'. She soon came to
know the look of the 'cheerful' bean-leaf that was likely
to co-operate and respond to her 'stimulations'—which
consisted of irritating the 'pulvinules' (little cushions at
the bottom of the leaflets) in a variety of ways.

There's little garden news. Ovenden has been strew-
ing the accumulated tea-leaves of many weeks over my
crocuses, which are just beginning to show. He says
they 'make them flower'; they certainly make them look
very nasty at the moment. And in a fortnight's time,
when they are due to flower any way, I shall doubtless
be greeted with, 'There, Sir! What did I tell you?'

By the way, I know you are writing under difficulties,
but I couldn't read—and would very much like to know
—whether that extremely unpleasant young friend of

yours, Dick Property, is 'living in sin' or 'living on gin'.
Tell me when you write.

February 14th

So you can now walk with only *one* supporter! which
have you dispensed with—the nurse or the house surgeon?

I think I now have clearer views about Susanna. She's
one of those simple souls who have interests beyond
their intelligences. Anything she can't understand—
which I fear is almost everything—she assumes, *omne
ignotum pro magnifico*, to be what she calls 'important'
(her favourite word). She's done so much work for me
in my garden that I've been on the look-out for some
way of repaying her more adequately than with buns;
so when she spoke enthusiastically of an 'important'

film that was just coming to London, I suggested she should dine with me and go to it afterwards. It's a French film called 'Off the rails' (in French, 'Deux et deux font cinq'), and the star is an Armenian actor named Aram Abramov—which was, of course, her main reason for wanting to see it.

Susanna accepted with alacrity, and I got David to join us: I couldn't face a *tête-à-tête*. I didn't prime him about her; I thought I'd let him puzzle her out for himself. The dinner at the White Tower—the nearest I could get to Armenian cuisine—was certainly 'important, Susanna eating her way through five courses including one that was genuinely Armenian and looked like sawdust. Delia had warned me that Susanna's conversation was sometimes disconcerting, and I'd had some evidence of this myself; but I must confess that I was shaken when suddenly, in the middle of a discussion about farming, she coolly remarked, 'I like very much the smell of sex'. David toyed nervously with a large olive; as for me, I didn't know which way to look. Feeling that she hadn't registered, she tried again: 'I like so much the smell of secks of corn.'

'Off the rails' was at Studio Eleven, where all the *avant-garde* films are now shown. I can't resist telling you the plot. It's the story of a young railway booking-office clerk, Charles, who is sentenced to two years' imprisonment for a theft he hasn't committed. He's replaced in his job by Charlot, who becomes what Charles would have become if he'd not been sent to prison. Charlot *is* Charles. They have the same parents, the same wife and children (but dressed to suit their different stations in life)—the roles being doubled by the same actors and actresses. Charlot becomes a railway magnate, Charles, after his release from prison, eventually gets taken on as a waiter in the dining-car of the *Train Bleu*.

The narrative is unfolded backwards and opens with the murder, in the dining-car, of Charlot (Aram Abramov) by Charles (also Aram Abramov). What with the trick photography, the infernal din of the train, and the reversed time-sequence, the plot is hard to follow. Whenever Charles or Charlot is meant to be 'thinking', various train-wheels are superimposed here and there on bits of his face, and the hubbub is doubled. The film closes with the premature birth of Charles-Charlot in a *wagon-lit*.

'Off the rails' was followed by a 'short' entitled 'It's better to walk' ('Apkutiksak Atsuilitsiarnermut Torartok'), a film made in Baffin Land entirely by Eskimos and released by Eskimo Experimental Inc. It was rather slow-moving; and since few if any of the audience can have understood Eskimo, it was a pity that the subtitles were printed in white on what was almost entirely snow.

David wrote me a nice letter of thanks. He observed that Susanna was 'a queer bird'; that the dinner was memorable; and of the main film, that he couldn't quite see what was gained by beginning the story at the wrong end. He is shaping well. As for Susanna, she arrived at Orchards the next morning with an armful of

traductions and a heartful of gratitude. When she
(eventually) left, I walked to the end of the drive with
her. It was raining, but I noticed that Colonel Moon
was pruning his roses; doesn't Saki say somewhere that
when a man prunes roses in the rain, one may be sure
that all isn't well with his home life?

Since then I've been sowing seeds in the greenhouse
by day and reading about them by night. I was amazed
to discover what a variety there is of seeds and fruit. The
seeds of the creeping goodyera, a little British orchid,
are so light that I could send you 14 million of them by
post for threepence, while the double coconut (the fruit
of the Seychelles palm) weighs about forty pounds and
takes ten years to ripen. There's the seed, the size of a
hazel-nut, of 'an Umbellifer indigenous to the High
Steppes of the East' which is so light that if it's laid on
the hand of a blindfold person he can't feel it, and (says
Sir Thomas Browne) 'the true seeds of Cypresse and
Rampions are indistinguishable by old eyes'.

Then the variety of shape and form. Some fruits are
winged; some look like little shaving-brushes, some like
parachutes or propellers. Some are as innocent-looking
as a pill, others as formidable as a miniature sword-fish
or porcupine. They may be soft as putty or hard as concrete. Some are sticky, others smooth and glossy as
polished mahogany (the horse-chestnut, for example).
There are some so boldly designed, so plastic in form,
that Henry Moore could learn from them. The seeds of
the Indian Lotus 'rattle in their sockets like teeth in the
jawbone of a skull'.

You know the capsule of the common poppy-bowl covered with a fluted lid supported by little pil-ters? What a model for the silversmith who wants to design a sugar-castor! The fruit of the willow-herb is simply fantastic—plumes like osprey feathers. And so are thistle-down and the parachute of the dandelion; no need to go further than the nearest hedgerow to find something that is quite wonderful under a magnifying-glass.

This year I'm sowing seeds of two climbing plants I haven't tried before—*Cobaea scandens* and *Calonyction aculeatum* (the moonflower)—and making yet another effort to succeed better with the blue morning glory. The seeds of the moonflower are the size of small peas and as hard as bullets. Having failed to 'nick' them with a razor blade I put them to soak for twenty-four hours in water. There are a number of ways in which hard, obstinate seeds can be encouraged to germinate: some can be frozen, some treated with boiling water, some with heat and cold alternately. Others may be corroded with acid or dipped into pure alcohol (nearly four hundred years ago Francis Bacon tried soaking seeds in claret). Some like being shaken up in a tin to bruise them. Some germinate best in the dark, others in the light; some germinate in a day or two, others take months or even years.

The embryo plant has to break out of the seed just as the chicken has to break out of the egg. Sir Edward Salisbury writes very well and clearly about germination in *The Living Garden*, and nicely illustrates the different ways in which embryo plants absorb the food 'placed by the parent plant as a sort of trading capital on which the young plant, when it grows, can earn compound interest'. In some (e.g. the broad bean) this food is absorbed by the baby plant before it passes the dormant state; in others (e.g. the guelder rose) the plant doesn't absorb the food until it begins to germinate:

> The difference is comparable to that between a baby going to sleep with a bottle of milk by its bedside, which it will promptly consume on waking, and a baby that drinks its bottle of milk before it goes to sleep. The food is equally there in both instances during sleep, but in the one outside the baby and in the other within.

I was sorry to discover that it isn't true that mummy wheat has been grown from grains found in Egyptian tombs. Gullible tourists have merely been defrauded: wheat grains remain 'viable' for twenty years at the most. Willow and poplar seeds are finished in a few days; the seed of the Indian lotus can germinate after remaining dormant for several hundred years.

How fascinating it all is! As Ruskin said of another aspect of plant life. 'I am astonished hourly, more and more, at the apathy and stupidity which have prevented me hitherto from learning the most simple facts at the base of this question.' Yet often the *explanation* of plant behaviour still eludes the scientist. For example, fresh seed of the Nottingham catchfly (*Silene nutans*) germinates better in the dark, whereas after two months' storage it germinates as readily in the light: but nobody seems to know why.

Your mother showed me the specialist's report—*most* encouraging, and I'm delighted. Also I'm so glad to hear that you've patched it up with McGrath; I always thought there couldn't be much wrong with a man who played the oboe *and* collected wild orchids!

February 22nd

I have just brought in a few celandines (I do it every February) and put them in a small purple and white cup on the window-sill, where they opened wide at once. Plenty of flowers are glossy, but do you know any, outside the buttercup family, that can be called *varnished*? (Odd that Wordsworth, who addressed three poems to the celandine, never thought of 'varnished'; Tennyson did.) You remember that game that children play: 'Do you like butter?' You couldn't play 'Do you like marmalade?' with a marigold or 'Do you like Burgundy?' with a begonia; bright though they are, they don't *reflect* their colours. I also admire the *independence* of the celandine, which has exactly as many petals as it feels inclined and refuses to be bullied by the botanists.

I've read somewhere that there's a memorial to Wordsworth on which the *greater* celandine has been engraved. As I'm sure you know, the greater celandine —the one that old Dürer painted so beautifully—is a poppy and nothing whatever to do with Wordsworth.

I noticed at the R.H.S. Show last year that Man has now tamed the lesser celandine, 'doubled' the flower, doubled its size, changed its colour and (I was told) checked its regrettable *wanderlust* and made it relatively border-trained. (It's certainly good that it can be controlled, for it really is hell when it gets into a bed.) I noticed also that Man was sending in a substantial bill for his improvements. So long as God continues to issue his celandine free, and so long as I have a bit of hedgerow for it to wander in, I shall save my pence.

Oh, if only people would really *look at* and *learn about* and *enjoy* common flowers, instead of whoring after nurserymen's novelties and other men's rarities, how much happier they would be! 'When gentle Spring, in sunshine clad, returns to your garden, what will she see?' asks a rose-grower's advertisement. 'The old familiar quarters she left three seasons ago?' Personally I very much hope so—once I've got it into shape. But the blurb continues, 'Why not redecorate your garden? Wield the rosy brush with verve and imagination— paint a fresh swathe of colour down the path, or stipple that wall with one of the new ever-blooming climbers.

Etch fresh laughter lines on old beds' faces with jaunty rows of miniatures, and prepare a mild reproach for fickle Spring's inconstancy, with cascades of weeping standards.' In other words, dig up your flourishing Madame Butterfly and replace it by a brick-redder than brick-red horror.

Of course, *some* of the new roses and other novelties are magnificent. But I wholeheartedly share Evelyn's indignation when he 'beheld a florist, or meaner gardener, transported at the casual discovery of a new little spot, double-leaf, streak or dash extraordinary in a Tulip, Anemonie, Carnation, Auricula or Amaranth, cherishing and calling it by his own name, raising the price of a single bulb to an enormous sum and priding himself as if he had found the Grand Elixir, or performed some notable achievement, and discovered a new country.' I once wrote an article on flowers which was set for dictation to the English students at Munich University. One student, I was told, spelt 'horticulture' 'haughtyculture' throughout. The haughtyculturist is a good name for the kind of person who is as terrified of growing last year's roses as is a woman of being seen in last year's hats.

To turn to quite another matter. Baby animals are irresistibly attractive to almost everyone (you've only got to see what happens in the cinema when a kitten or a puppy appears on the screen), but baby plants—I mean seedlings, not tiny alpines—don't excite people in the least, do they? I suppose the trouble with baby plants is that they don't frolic and gambol; but at least they don't do any of those regrettable things that baby animals do—chewing, upsetting, wetting things and being thoroughly destructive and unco-operative. Give me a cobaea seedling every time!

All of which is a prelude to telling you that my cobaeas and moonflowers have both already germinated, and I'm far more excited than I would be if Mrs. Benham's spaniel had pupped. I stood the pots, in which I'd sown the moonflower seed, on the radiator, and within forty-eight hours the first seedling appeared. It broke through the soil with its arched back, and in a few days had pulled its crumpled head free from the earth. Now I have half-a-dozen sturdy little plants, each with its pair of flat, shiny seed-leaves. The cobaeas did much the same, only they took rather longer. Meanwhile I've been trying to find out what I can about the two plants.

The moonflower is a tropical climber of both hemispheres—a large, white, night-flowering, sweet-scented convolvulus that used to be called *Ipomoea Bona-nox*. 'Calonyction' comes from Greek words meaning 'beauty' and 'night'—in fact, *kalenukta* is the modern Greek for 'goodnight'—and 'aculeatum' (having prickles) refers to the spurs on the stem; so the plant would seem to be fairly sensibly named, though the spurs aren't in fact prickly.

Clifford, who was Burgomaster of Amsterdam in the early part of the eighteenth century, grew it in one of his greenhouses at Hartekamp. He sowed the seed in mid-April, and by early June of the same year it had shot up to twelve feet; but he didn't get it to flower.

Lord Bute introduced it into England in 1773. I've only seen photographs of it, but it sounds exciting.

Cobaea is another rampant climber, with cup-and-saucer flowers which open pale green and gradually turn purple, and there's also a white form. A native of southern Mexico, it was brought to Madrid in 1791, and reached England about ten years later. Oddly enough it belongs to the Polemonium family, of which the only members you probably know are the polemonium itself (Jacob's ladder) and the phlox: it couldn't look less like either of them, but no doubt the botanists, who group their plants by physiological rather than by superficial resemblance, know best. Father Cobo, after whom it was named, was a Jesuit missionary and naturalist in Mexico and Peru in the first half of the seventeenth century, and had no more to do with the plant than had Dr. Fuchs with the fuchsia or the Rev. Adam Buddle with the buddleia. (Ruskin predicted that the day would come when 'men of science will think their names disgraced, instead of honoured, by being used to barbarize nomenclatures'; it hasn't come yet—though in this case one can't of course blame Cobo.)

I first saw cobaea covering the whole of an enormous wall at Orotava, in the Canary Islands. It's said to be able to grow as much as 200 feet from seed in a single season, but there's no danger of it doing that in the open in England. It will be interesting to see how far it does manage to scramble.

I'll post you the two books you ask for; I happen to have one of them, and Usher had *Plants with Personality*.

P.S. Your mother has sent me a label of instructions off a house-plant she had bought. It reads:

This repays care and attention. Keep in a warm room, away from all draughts, throughout the winter. Feed regularly and liberally, and give plenty of water as soon as signs of dryness appear. Can be trimmed into shape at any time.

She had changed 'water' to 'whisky' and added at the bottom, 'It might be *you*!' Pretty offensive, I thought.

February 29th

Today, in a normal year, we would have moved into March. As Mrs. Benham said this morning, 'I wonder what made them add the extra day to February when they could just as easily have added it to June.'

Tremendous news that you are to be let out of prison! How lucky that you have a conveniently-placed aunt and can live with her while you are getting the physio-therapy at the hospital. I'm sure you will be wise to stay up there as long as you go on with the treatment; you seem to be in first-rate hands and it would be madness to start chopping and changing. How nice of McGrath to send you those flowers to welcome you on your arrival!

I've had a large cocktail party—one of those 'working-off' parties which the guests dislike almost as much as the host. I warned Delia and Humphrey what they would be in for, said that both Mrs. Puttenham and Mrs. Moon would probably be there and that I'd quite understand if they'd rather keep away. But Delia said, 'No, we'll come. I'll enjoy seeing that awful woman slumming.' 'That awful woman' is always Mrs. Putten-ham, Mrs. Moon being less detested because, in her maddening way, she does do good in the village. (It fascinates me that Delia's apparently unbounded kind-liness has a boundary after all!)

I think that everybody I've mentioned to you at one time or another in my letters was there, and about a dozen others who needn't be specified. Mrs. Benham had contrived a lot of nice oddments to eat, and I mixed the drinks strong. Except for a quadrangular dog-fight at the height of the party (the Admiral's bull-terrier, Delia's retrievers and the Stringers' green mongrel) there was no major calamity. Humphrey, the Admiral and Colonel Moon were the heroes of the dog-fight. All

I

three were terribly brave; but Colonel Stringer ran off to his house to fetch pepper, timing it so nicely that he got back exactly when everything was over. I couldn't resist asking Delia whether that was what she meant when she said that he'd be 'a tower of strength in a crisis'. She admitted he'd done pretty badly (and so, for that matter, had I: but really, people who own dogs should deal with them); but she added, 'Anyhow, Darling, you *can't* deny that he's *terribly* good-looking.' 'I most certainly can,' I said. 'I find him repulsive. He's like a rather *passé* gigolo.'

I had only a couple of minutes' conversation with Mrs. Puttenham, most of which was devoted to her expression of sympathy for me for having to live in such squalor. 'You can't really do anything with a house like this or like Mr. Lovell's. You should pull it down and build something more convenient. It would pay you in the end. I had to spend six thousand pounds on modernizing the Hall when we came—but then it's a house worth spending money on. Where's Oliver? It's time we were going. Oh, there he is! Who's that Chelsea type with a beard he's talking to?'

I said he was a very talented young pianist I'd wanted Oliver to meet. Mrs. Puttenham expressed the opinion that Oliver already wasted far too much time on music—'gramophone records and all that sort of thing', and hoped I wasn't encouraging him. I said I was; that he was very musical and ought to be encouraged. Mrs. Puttenham didn't answer, but called to Oliver to come at once.

The Moons had already left and the air seemed suddenly clearer. Delia came over to me and whispered, 'Darling, do congratulate me! I wasn't rude to either of them—not once. And now could I have one small and very weak drink and then we must go home.'

Just at that moment, when I thought the party was breaking up, some people called Drake arrived; they live the other side of Horsham, and I'd quite forgotten about them. Dorothy Drake was full of apologies and rather unconvincing descriptions of nightmare traffic jams. Delia said, 'I can never understand what Lewis Carroll meant by "jam tomorrow and jam yesterday—but never jam today".' Mrs. Stringer, who had joined us, thought hard and then said suddenly: 'Don't you think he might perhaps have meant *the kind of jam you eat?*'

I suppose that, as such parties go, it went off all right. I dined off the funeral baked meats and then helped Mrs. Benham clear up the mess.

Are you, my dear Flora, a *crocodile?* You will answer —quite correctly, but for the wrong reason—'No'; for you didn't know that, according to (the admittedly unreliable) Fuller, 'crocodile' means 'crocus-dreader'. I'm terribly glad that I went a bust on species crocuses in the autumn, for now I'm reaping my reward. Though I've got about a dozen different kinds, and in particular some of the lovely *chrysanthus* strains, *C. Tomasinianus* and *C. aureus* remain my real favourites. Both naturalize well—so well in fact that plantsmen, who have a dread of any plant that makes itself at home, are crocodiles where *Tomasinianus* is concerned and warn one that it is liable to come up all over the place. To see *Tomasinianus* 'coming up all over the place' is the nearest thing I know to seeing an alpine slope covered with *Crocus albiflorus*—and that is almost the most glorious sight that the Alps have to offer in early spring. In fact, *Tomasinianus* is its Dalmatian equivalent, and for some strange reason it seems to like the English. Patrick Synge calls them 'Tommies', which I won't; and Roy Hay, 'Tomasin's crocuses', which they aren't: Muzio de Tommasini, who collected them in Dalmatia, was an Italian botanist whose name was—and apparently intentionally!—misspelt when the flower was christened.

Aureus, says Farrer, 'has the terrible responsibility of being parent to many Fat Boys of the garden and grass plots.' But it's the most golden, the most Western, and one of the most historical of the yellow crocuses. It's the crocus that 'broke out like fire' at the feet of blind old Oedippus as he groped his way home to Colonus. Gerard, who got it from Jean Robin of Paris, described its flowers as 'of a most shining yellow colour, seeming afar off to be a hot glowing cole of fire'. There's a fine picture of it in Sibthorp's *Flora Graeca*.

Ever your very affectionate godfather

Wilfrid Sharp

MARCH

March 3rd

My dearest Flora,

I'm most *awfully* sorry to hear you've had a bit of a relapse. Your aunt wrote very fully; I gather that neither Arbuthnot nor McGrath are in the least seriously worried, and that such ups and downs often happen. So *don't* be discouraged; you've done so splendidly so far. It was probably the excitement of being released from hospital; and it can't be anything very bad if they don't want you to go back there.

I have just bought two pocket lenses, one magnifying ten times and the other five, and I can't begin to tell you what a joy they are. When I 'did' science at Bedales we used a microscope, but it had almost always to be directed at the *curious* rather than at the *beautiful*—I mean, at things such as a fly's leg. Also, even though it was a low-power microscope, the magnification was greater than what is suitable to show the beauty of a flower, just as the magnification of an ordinary magnifying glass (the kind that lies on the writing-table, which

is all that I've had in the past) is not enough. With a
× 10 or × 5 lens one can see the amazing subtleties of
texture and colour and form of plants.

Do you realize what '× 10' means? It means that the
linear measurements are multiplied by 10, and there-
for the *area* by 100. So a daisy from the lawn becomes
the size of a tea-plate. But it isn't simply a question of
size: with the lenses you can see the minute glistening
particles (the cells?) which compose the petals. You can
see the astonishing refinement of the feathering on the
petal of a crocus, the marvellous veining of an iris, the
incredible intricacies of anther, style and pollen. Even
the colours seem to be intensified.

The 'heart' of a flower is of course the sexual parts
of a plant, and Ruskin strongly denounced what he
called 'vexatious and vicious peeping' into their private
lives:

It is very possible, indeed, that the recent phrensy
for the investigation of digestive and reproductive
operations in plants may by this time have furnished
the microscopic malice of botanists with providen-
tially disgusting reasons, or demoniacally nasty
necessities, for every possible spur, spike, jag, sting,
rent, blotch, flaw, freckle, filth, or venom, which can
be detected in the construction, or distilled from the
dissolution, of vegetable organism. But with these
obscene processes and prurient apparitions the gentle
and happy scholar of flowers has nothing whatever to
do. . . .'

What Ruskin found obscene, a Dutch seventeenth-century naturalist and philosopher found profane. Jan Swammerdam, turning the recently discovered microscope upon insects and plants, was so overwhelmed by what he saw that he went mad and smashed it to pieces, considering it a sacrilege to unveil what God had obviously intended to remain hidden. I don't know what Ruskin thought about the use of a pocket lens, but I'd think the worse of him if I found that he condemned it along with the microscope. In fact, in spite of Ruskin, I'm getting a small dissecting microscope as well, because I can't see as much as I want of the structure of grains of pollen and so on.

Delia drove me over to lunch with Charlotte Bonham-Carter to see her aconites—a great sloping hillside of gold. She's another splendid person whom you must meet when you come here—one of those real 'originals' who brighten this drab age.

There's to be a concert in the Village Hall in aid of the Conservative Association—the one activity which brings Delia (very reluctantly) into joint harness with Mrs. Puttenham and Mrs. Moon. The Puttenham is to sing at it. I've told Delia more than once that I'm not interested in politics, and could at best be described (and have been) as 'an unthinking Conservative', but she has insisted upon my going with her. I admit I'm curious to hear Mrs. P., whom Delia says 'isn't nearly as bad as you'd expect'. And anyhow, it's impossible to refuse Delia anything.

Incidentally, Helen has told me that Mrs. Puttenham

has given Mrs. Wishart (a rather pathetic and impoverished widow in the village) a cheque for twenty pounds to help her through a difficult period. Helen got it straight from Mrs. Wishart, who had promised not to mention it to anyone but who let it out by mistake. I find it hard to believe, but Helen swears it's true. I asked if I could tell Delia, but Helen said, No, she really oughtn't to have passed it on to me.

March 10th

I was enormously relieved to get your cheerful letter this morning, telling me that the pain had completely gone. No more relapses in future, please!

Of course I'll be of any help I can with your article on Forsythia; let me know if you want me to do any research for you, and send it along when you've sketched it out. Vita Sackville-West says somewhere that it's the hardest thing in the world to write about flowers.

What she means, of course, is to write *well* about flowers—and nobody does it better than she; you must read her *Some Flowers* if you haven't already done so. The trouble is that almost everything that can possibly be said about the obvious flowers—and what could be more obvious than forsythia?—has already been said a hundred times, and I don't suppose you'll be able to do much more than repeat it yet again.

But you don't tell me what paper your article is for, and that makes all the difference. Anyhow, begin with a general statement: 'There is no more charming shrub for the spring garden than the forsythia (*Forsythia* × *intermedia* var. *spectabilis*);' put that in—to show you're a real botanist. 'In March and April its boughs are hung with . . .' And here you must pause to consider the 'brow' of your reader: is it to be, 'inodorous panicles of flavous inflorescence', 'a riot of golden bell-shaped blossoms', or 'a profusion of dainty little golden bells whose fairy carillon is the joyful harbinger of spring'? Make your choice.

Follow this up with some general information about soil, planting, pruning, etc. Mention one or two of the species. And if you still have to spin it out you could do worse than put in a line or two about Forsyth himself. All this can be got from standard reference books. In fact, I often wonder why the newspapers think it worth their while to publish, year after year, the same old stuff —and stuff that's to be found in any gardening book. I was for a time the Gardening Correspondent of the *Sunday* ——, so I know all about it. It was easy money and, since I could count on there being daffodils in March, I could write my articles in advance. This gave me a tremendous advantage over most of my colleagues.

But I must tell you of an amusing thing that happened. I'd written a very colourful article on the effectiveness of massed *Tulipa Fosteriana*—the whole thing being an effort of the imagination because at the time I'd only a small back-garden. So picture my feelings when I got a letter from the Secretary of a Hertfordshire Gardening Club asking if she could bring over two coach-loads of members to see my tulips!

Perhaps my articles weren't good enough. Or perhaps it was just that I didn't give my readers what they wanted—which was the information most of them already had in their own bookshelves. They wanted to know about fertilizers and early potatoes; I told them too much about the history of the introduction of the dahlia. Anyhow I got the sack. It was a pity; I was enjoying it.

I went with Delia to the Conservative concert. You can guess what most of it was like—boy scouts and girl guides, the Church choir (one or two Labour abstainers), a little play by the Women's Institute produced by Helen, and so on. Six boy scouts did some acrobatics which consisted chiefly of their standing on their heads, or on each other's, for an unnecessarily long time. It awoke memories of disagreeable hours in the gymnasium at school. I always disliked standing on my head; the sensations it produced convinced me that the Almighty never intended such a posture to be at all permanent, and I used to feel it was a pity that He hadn't arranged for us to be stamped at birth with 'THIS SIDE UP WITH CARE'. Even boy scouts look best the right way up.

The play had been written by one of the members of the W.I. It was a very long sort of historical pageant, but not as historical as it imagined. The Egyptians, it is said, when attired for a feast, had little birds in their garlands to peck them and keep them awake: I could have done with one or two myself. But I was glad I woke up in time to see Susanna and Helen as the Virgin Queen and Sir Walter Raleigh respectively. There followed one of the witches' scenes from Macbeth, the witches played by Mrs. Upnately, Mrs. Muchrather and Miss Tinklechild, with Mr. Trump, the sexton, as Macbeth (we have some splendid local names).

The *bonne bouche* (or *coup de grâce*, as Delia rather unkindly called it) was Mrs. Puttenham, draped in a Union Jack, singing 'Land of Hope and Glory'— through which no Egyptian could have slumbered. For to my great surprise I found that she had a magnificent, but of course neglected, 'Clara Butt' voice: nobody had told me that she'd once trained as a singer. She's totally unmusical; but so, after all, are nine contraltos out of ten. Somebody should have told the architect of the Hall that it was a mistake to put the lavatory just off-stage; the flushing, especially during the *coup de grâce*, was distracting—and Delia thought deliberate.

Chandler had massed the front of the stage with blue and white cinerarias, and Mrs. Puttenham's scarlet dress, very visible under the Union Jack, provided the extra red. I went back to supper with Delia afterwards and we had a good laugh over it all. I hear they took eleven pounds odd, which should very nearly cover the expenses.

The Moons have planted an oak on the village green to celebrate their silver wedding. 'A few friends' were invited to the ceremony. I couldn't go and Delia wasn't asked, but Helen was present and reported. Mrs. Moon, in her best bless-this-ship-and-all-who-sail-in-her voice, made a patriotic hearts-of-oak speech and cut the first sod, leaving the colonel to do all the work. A few days later the oak was uprooted by hooligans—but not before Eric, who chanced to pass through the village, had identified it as *Quercus castaneifolia*, a most *un*-British species which grows in the Caucasus and even behind the Iron Curtain.

P.S. I've just seen golden privet described in a catalogue as 'bottled sunshine'—a phrase usually reserved for the more expensive Sauternes. You might pinch the idea for forsythia.

March 18th

'I've been reading . . .'—I feel as though all my letters begin like that! But it's true: I've been reading two of Robert Fortune's books with great pleasure. He was a Scot who was sent to the Far East by the R.H.S. in 1842 to collect plants—which he did very successfully, among them being the winter jasmine and the Japanese anemone.

He has a pleasant description of Howqua's famous garden at Canton, and the notices posted up in it to regulate the behaviour of visitors. A fruit-tree near the Library of Verdant Purity (i.e., the summerhouse) bore a label inscribed, 'Ramblers here *will be excused* plucking the fruit of this tree'. At the entrance to the garden was

A CAREFUL AND EARNEST NOTICE

This garden earnestly requests that visitors will spit betle outside the railing, and knock the ashes of pipes also outside.

Isn't this far nicer than NO SMOKING, DO NOT SPIT, and so on? And I've still to see a fruit-tree labelled PLEASE PICK.

Have you ever bothered to read any of the instructions for the behaviour of visitors, posted up in the London parks? For example, Clause 3, sub-section 13 of those in St. James's Park forbids the unauthorized 'erecting, or using, of any apparatus for the transmission, reception, reproduction, or amplification of sound, speech or images by electrical or mechanical means', but in a generous afterthought excludes from the £5 penalty 'apparatus designed and used as an aid to defective hearing'. The Germans are still more thorough. A notice at the entrance to the public gardens at Rothenburg, in Bavaria, informs intending visitors that they may not enter if drunk, verminous, or suffering from an infectious disease; that they may not (among other things) hold meetings, distribute pamphlets, erect tents, ski, toboggan, play football, mow the grass, sit down except in such places as are appointed for sitting, or play in the sand-pit if over the age of twelve. In the Acropolis things are even worse: one cannot 'take improper pictures, sing or make loud noises, or introduce food or animals'. But in the Istanbul Public Gardens there is, I am told, a 'lovers' corner' labelled 'Flirtation permitted here'. Give me the Turks every time!

Returning to Howqua's fruit-tree—fruit-stealers, and plant-robbers in general, are a real menace in this country, and sheer hooligans still more so. But it's nothing new in the West: more than three hundred years ago a keen horticulturist smeared the edge of his robe with gum and so collected seed of a rare anemone from the garden of his Parisian rival, Maître Bachelier. I can't help wondering sometimes how Eric gets his rareties; he never says.

Which reminds me that perhaps I have been maligning the paper boy. I thought it was *he* who pulled up my plant labels, but on the wireless this morning I learnt that somebody had found a jackdaw's nest entirely composed of six-inch lead labels bent to shape. We've lots of jackdaws here. Incidentally, what a nest one of Eric Leighton's jackdaws could build!

Delia rang up a few days ago and said, 'Darling, I've just heard from Helen that Mrs. Moon is away, so it's a *wonderful* chance to have the colonel to dinner and I want you to come—on Thursday, and don't dress. And do you know, the first three days I suggested he was already dining out! It just *shows*, doesn't it!'

I'd liked the colonel from the first time I'd met him, but I thought him a bit dull. I couldn't have been more wrong. The Lovells' charm and hospitality, and the blessed absence of Mrs. Moon, worked a miracle; he became gay, carefree, and twenty years younger. In the end Humphrey and I almost carried him to the piano, where he sang some Purcell and Handel (not terribly well) to his own accompaniment. Helen was there too, and a nice woman called Jill Harrison whom I hadn't met before. Delia said to Jill, 'It's maddening; I meant to remind you to bring your clarinet, and I forgot.' However, Jill had in fact brought it, and she and Helen played some Brahms very well indeed.

It was after midnight before we left. I heard the colonel saying to Delia, 'You mustn't tell my wife I've been singing; she doesn't like me to.' Delia answered— rather bravely, I thought—'Darling, don't take any notice of her; she doesn't appreciate you. You must practise every day and then do a duet with Mrs. Puttenham at the next Conservative concert. *And* I won't tell your wife I'm kissing you goodnight!'

Mr. Peters has moved his gnomery to the side of his garden, where it doesn't show so much, and planted a monkey-puzzle in the place where it stood—six feet from the house; would it be kind to tell him that it will one day bring the house down, or will he then put the gnomery back? In the branches of this little tree he has placed a toy monkey from Woolworth's; the monkey certainly wears a puzzled look—possibly because there are no monkeys in southern Chili, where *Araucaria araucana* comes from.

It's a shame that the monkey-puzzle has become a joke; a big, well-grown, well-placed specimen can look magnificent. In the early years of the last century it was described as 'the finest plant in the world'; but now it's folly to plant one, because one's successor will very likely have 'taste' and therefore cut it down. A friend of mine—a rather pompous little Classical don—bought a house with a splendid monkey-puzzle in the garden; he immediately had it axed, and turned the stump into a sundial which he inscribed, ARAUCARIA SED HORA CARIOR.

When I was in London on Monday I bought a coat 'off the peg'. On unpacking it I discovered that it was ticketed '45 Outsize Portly'! That should make a good title for the penultimate (I hope) chapter of my autobiography—which I've been working on, very secretly, for some time past, though I very much doubt whether I shall ever have the courage to publish it. It involves too many people who are still living.

No more; the post is going.

March 25th

I *am* sorry! You took me *too* literally about the Forsythia. I thought you'd see I wasn't being entirely serious. I will be frank: as it stands, the article *simply won't do*. May I attack it piecemeal? Take this:

The season generally associated with the Forsythia is the spring, the blossoms tend to appear at the beginning or in the middle of March, but in an early season they may already be open by the end of February or the beginning of March, while in a late season one may have to wait until the end of March or the beginning of April for the first blossoms to appear.

Seventy words (and no stop but a comma) to say so little! At twopence a word (I think you said) you're simply robbing Lord K. of ten or eleven shillings. I

K

would substitute for the whole lot, 'Forsythia usually flowers in March'—for which I'm afraid you'll only get tenpence! Observant gardeners will probably have noticed that shrubs tend to flower earlier in an early season, and the reverse; if they haven't, they'd better take up knitting instead. Or this:

> Remember that what is now a small shrub will in the course of years become a larger one, and it is therefore desirable to allow adequate space for ultimate expansion. In this respect prevention rather than cure is the objective to be aimed at and constantly kept in mind when planting.

Now all you mean is, 'Don't plant too close'; and it would have been more helpful if you'd told us, in feet, what the 'ultimate expansion' is likely to be. And for sheer flatulence—forgive me!—it would be hard to beat the following:

> The precise position for the planting of the Forsythia in the shrubbery must always remain a matter of personal choice. Some will prefer one position, some another.

I was about to object to, 'Their early-flowering habit and floriferousness make them valuable shrubs for any garden', but I find you've lifted the sentence verbatim from the R.H.S. Dictionary. (How on earth did you get hold of it? I feel sure your aunt hasn't got a copy.) None the less, do go slow with words like 'habit' and 'floriferousness', and watch out for clichés and wordy windiness and that kind of mock-scientific writing which ruins nine gardening books out of ten and ninety-nine gardening articles out of a hundred. You write, 'Forsythia is tolerant of a very wide range of soils and aspects'. All you mean is, 'Forsythia will grow almost anywhere'. Why not say so?

Flora dear, I *do* hope all this won't send your temperature up again. But when people ask me to be frank, I'm afraid I generally am. You have so many talents, and possibly writing isn't going to turn out to be one of them. However, *don't* give up after one failure. Shall I send you, from time to time, examples (both good and bad) for you to study? It might be helpful. Here, for a start, is a fine specimen of the over-lush—Eleanour Sinclair Rohde on the Madonna lily—which I came across yesterday:

Upborne on a slender stem, arrayed in lustrous sheen whiter than snow, and with only her delicate orange-golden stamens for a crown, what other flower offers so rare a vision of royal glory and even more royal humility? And her scent, though of surpassing sweetness, is like the radiance of the flower, elusive and not of this world . . . the scent of ages yet to come and of beauties and splendours yet unrevealed. From those glorious trumpets float melodies at one with the music of the spheres, and which must surely have ascended in unison with the morning stars when they sang together. . . .'[1]

[1] *The Scented Garden* (Medici Soc., n.d.).

A woman sitting behind me in the bus today (I went to Kew) said to her neighbour, pointing to a *Magnolia soulangiana*, 'Hasn't that cherry got big flowers!' I was reminded of the story, told by Lecky, of how Tennyson persuaded a town-bred woman who was visiting him at Freshwater, that 'a common daisy was a peculiar kind of rhododendron only found in the Isle of Wight'.

The following, from the *Gardeners Chronicle* for 1863, interested me as showing that Teddy boys and other hooligans are nothing new. When a certain Colonel Tighe opened his house and gardens on Sundays to the public, 'parties arrived reeling drunk . . . and the plants were knocked about the passages in a manner which no one would believe without having seen it; plants were pulled out of the beds . . . and I was abused to the extreme for not allowing dancing to take place on the lawn. On Mondays the seats have to be cleaned of porter . . .' This, commented the writer, was the result of trying to 'elevate the working classes'.

Ever your very affectionate godfather

Wilfrid Sharp

P.S. Here are the titles of two lectures given recently at botanical conferences: 'The Physiology of Sex Attraction in the Cucumber' and 'Apoplexy in the Apricot'. No, I *haven't* made them up!

APRIL

April 1st

My dearest Flora,

It's sounded all the morning as though a battle were raging in Dewbury; but it's only the Admiral, who, having no more trees on which to expend his surplus energy, has declared war on grey squirrels, bullfinches and other local pests and is moving from garden to garden slaughtering. I hailed him for a whisky; I enjoy his conversation, which is always so gloriously unexpected. He said, 'I suppose you've heard about poor Pwiscilla Moon?—a fwightful twagedy.' 'No,' I said; 'what's happened?' 'Murdered! A howwid gorwy mess. Sergeant Cwopper is in there now.' He gave me the fullest details: the colonel under suspicion, his finger-prints found on the revolver, his attempted suicide. . . . 'But this is awful,' I said. 'Is there nothing we can do to help? Oughtn't we to go round and see?' 'I wouldn't if I were you.' The Admiral chuckled: 'Haven't you forgotten it's Apwil the First?' The trouble with the Admiral is that he's never really grown up, and has to live in a world of fantasy.

I'm sorry about the article, and *thank you* for forgiving me. But you say you find my letters 'a bit sarcastic'. O my dear Flora—*surely* you've known me long enough to understand me and read between the lines! Do you mean *all* my letters, or just the teasing bits about forsythia? I now begin to regret having criticized the article; if I'd simply said how nice it was, you'd have been perfectly happy and ten pounds the richer. But really, you shouldn't have asked me to be frank if you didn't mean me to be. As for the sarcasm—well, that's the way I write, and you must take it or leave it.

As to what to read with profit—why not start with Ruskin? There are splendid passages in *Proserpina* (which I'll send you when I find the energy to pack it up)—for example, the piece about the poppy:

I have in my hand a small red poppy which I gathered on Whit Sunday on the palace of the Caesars. It is an intensely simple, intensely floral, flower. All silk and flame: a scarlet cup, perfect-edged all round, seen among the wild grass far away, like a burning coal fallen from heaven's altars. You cannot have a more complete, a more stainless, type of flower absolute; inside and outside, *all* flower. No sparing of colour anywhere—no outside coarsenesses—no interior secrecies; open as the sunshine that creates it; fine-finished on both sides, down to the extremest point of insertion on its narrow stalk; and robed in the purple of the Caesars. . . . We usually think of a poppy as a coarse flower; but it is the most transparent and

delicate of all the blossoms of the field. The rest—
nearly all of them—depend on the *texture* of their
surfaces for colour. But the poppy is painted *glass*;
it never glows so brightly as when the sun shines
through it. Wherever it is seen—against the light or
with the light—always, it is a flame, and warms the
wind like a blown ruby. . . .'

Ruskin quarrelled with the botanists and in his irri-
tation wrote a deal of nonsense. But how he could *write*!
If you compare this with E.S.R. on the Madonna lily
you'll see what I mean.

I've been trying to find out about how to keep cut-
flowers alive as long as possible. The principal rules
seem to be pretty obvious: take off the bottom leaves
and put the flowers in water as soon as possible; keep
them as cool as you can, and at all events in a cool room
overnight; change the water and recut the stems as
often as time and energy allow. As for myself, I admit
I have the time; but my energy only extends to keeping
the pot more or less filled up with water.

Potassium permanganate, aspirins or pennies in the
water do about equal damage to the bacteria and the
plant tissues and are therefore more or less useless.
Hammering the ends of stems helps the flower to
absorb water—but also bacteria; burning the ends discourages the absorption of bacteria—but also of water.
However, there now seems to be a new possibility, not
yet properly explored: the spraying of an almost invisible film of liquid latex to reduce the loss of water by

evaporation. I believe the Americans are working on this at the moment.

Patrick Synge has been over and has given me some excellent advice about the garden; he's also promised me one or two plants in the autumn. Then Graham Thomas turned up with some white stylosas he knew I was wanting, and inspected everything as thoroughly as if I had been National Trust. He was very interested in my rarer trees and shrubs.

No more for the present. Mrs. Benham has just sounded the gong and I get very sour looks if I'm even a second late. At the moment I'm thankful if I get anything to eat at all, because her very pretty niece, who spent a fortnight here and broke the heart of every young man in the village, has been chosen as Beauty Queen of Wolverhampton. Mrs. Benham can think, and talk, of nothing else, and is determined to go there for the 'coronation' and subsequent orgies. No doubt I shall then have to cook for myself—which will be even worse, for you know what a mug I am at it.

Later. Here is an exercise for you. Translate the following passage from botanese into English: 'When florescence is terminated, the bulb foliage of narcissi naturalized in grass should be permitted to remain until photosynthesis is concluded.' I'm all for gardeners gardening; but if they want to *write* about gardening, then I think they ought to learn to write English.

April 6th

Mrs. Moon (who *would* be called Priscilla—but I re-fuse to call her by that or any other Christian name) burst into my garden yesterday morning through our dividing hedge—which she has never been invited to do —and asked for flowers for the church. She asked politely and pleadingly: my forsythias and *Prunus blireiana* were ahead of hers; 'just a snippet or two, and a few daffies', etc. I was on the point of leaving for London; in a moment of insanity, and also as a gesture of reconciliation (because she knows I dislike her), I told her to help herself, and lent her a *small* pair of secateurs to impose a limit on her cutting.

I ought, of course, to have remembered that women like Mrs. Moon must be treated like Hitler. What I had intended as appeasement was interpreted as weak-ness. I came home to find my garden stripped. Mrs. Moon's idea of 'a snippet or two' of forsythia was the top half of several six-foot shrubs I'd planted in the autumn; she must have used a saw to cut them through. The same with the prunus—three or four great boughs hacked off that lovely tree near the sunk garden: it'll take it at least three years to recover its shape. As for the daffodils . . .

I was so angry that I drank two strong whiskies and went straight round and told her what I thought of her. Oh! I know what I should have done: I should have gone off and communed for a while with my tulip-tree. For 'It is hardly possible,' wrote 'Flora' (not you, I fear!) in *The Floricultural Cabinet* for 1844, 'to contemplate this noble tree, without having all sordid and angry passions driven from the breast, and exchanged for those of peace and philanthropy.' But I didn't, and I'm afraid I was very rude indeed; hints and sarcasm are wasted on pachyderms like Mrs. Moon.

She went very white and attempted to justify herself. They *were* rather big snippets—but then the church vases were rather big vases; one had to 'mass' daffodils to get any effect; if I went round to the church I'd see how pretty it all looked, and so on. I couldn't trust myself to answer. I turned and walked out of the house, slamming (I regret to say) the front door.

In fact it made me so angry that I found I couldn't sleep. So, stimulated by the Ruskin I'd been copying out for you, I got up, put on a dressing-gown, and started to read about poppies. An hour later, 'drowsed with the fume' of this literary opiate, I went back to bed and was asleep in a moment.

I've always had a very soft spot for poppies, starting with that little alpine one with finely cut grey leaves and flowers like acid-drops. The Iceland poppy too, which also runs the whole colour-gamut of citrous fruit drinks and grows so far north that an Arctic explorer once said he hoped to find it at the Pole. Bless, also, the Rev. W. Wilks for bothering to notice a white-edged corn-poppy in a field at Shirley and breeding from it the lovely Shirley strains.

But I think the oriental poppy—not pink or white but flaming red—is the most exciting of them all. Tournefort found it near Erzerum, in Armenia (I must remember to tell Susanna) in about 1700, and I collected it on the slopes of Mt. Demavend in northern Persia. As for the opium poppy—did you know that it used to be grown commercially in England a hundred and fifty years ago, and that 'loddy' (laudanum) made from it was 'much used instead of tea by the poorer class of females in Manchester'?

Plantsmen are unkind about the Welsh poppy (you should hear Eric on the subject!); it ought to be honoured, not only for its exquisite luminous yellow, but for being the only meconopsis to have strayed out of Asia. Farrer, though he admits to a sneaking affection for it, says that to let it into the rock garden is 'a catholic charity so complete as to verge upon the maudlin'. In fact, the best people have no use for a meconopsis unless it's blue or pink. But Ruskin loved the Welsh poppy, and called it the crosslet poppy and wouldn't call it a meconopsis—which, he said, only meant a 'poppaceous' plant and was in any case 'barbarous Greek'. But I'm sure he would have hated that orange variety—*and* the double form. Single flowers are often (though not always) the best: think of the double day lily, kerria, tulip and daffodil, for example.

Incidentally, Kingdon Ward has some admirable stuff about double flowers in *The Romance of Gardening*. 'Improved' plants are really *sick* plants, he says—plants tortured as geese are tortured to produce *pâté de foie gras*. Double flowers are flowers overfed until their reproductive organs no longer function: 'a Paeony, for example, is neither more nor less than a eunuch. A Rose by any other name would smell as sweet, and would be equally impotent.' But he assures us that plants, even if they have feelings, are without consciousness; and 'even the British people, swept by periodic gusts of sentimental sickness . . . have not yet thought fit to organize a society for the prevention of cruelty to plants'.

But back to our poppies. Of course you know the horned poppy—*Glaucium flavum*—that gay, sprawling plant of the seashore, much connected in my mind with Aldeburgh. Here is a curious story about it, as reported in 1698 to the Royal Society:

A certain person made a pye of the roots of this plant, supposing them to be roots of Eryngium [sea holly], of which he had before eaten pyes which were very pleasant, and eating it while it was hot, became delirious, and having voided a stool in a white chamber-pot, fancied it to be gold, breaking the pot in pieces, and desiring what he imagined as gold might be preserved as such.

To finish with poppies on a pleasanter note, here is the German traveller, Karl Moritz, who visited England in 1782, on the subject of English bread-and-butter:

The slices of bread and butter which they give you with your tea are as thin as poppy leaves [i.e. petals], But there is another kind of bread and butter usually eaten with tea, which is toasted by the fire, and is incomparably good. This is called 'toast'.

This morning Colonel Moon, who was not at home when I went round yesterday, called to apologize for his wife's behaviour. He said nothing that was technically disloyal; but I knew what he meant, and he knew that I knew what he meant. And it was this: 'We are both men—both members of the weaker sex. We know to our cost that all women are impossible, and how fortunate you are to be free! My wife is the most impossible of all women. I've endured forty years of hell. I quelled, almost single-handed, a mutiny at Chinpore; but I've never quelled Priscilla . . .'

My heart went out to him. I longed to say, 'You keep a muzzle in the hall; then why not use it? Stand up to her. Hit back, and hit extremely hard; that's the only thing such women understand.' But of course he's left it far too late.

And now there has come a warm letter of thanks from the Rector. He has heard that all those lovely flowers are from me. He has never seen the church looking so beautiful—'quite like a florist's shop'. He is deeply grateful for my generosity, which he fears must have left my garden very bare.

It has.

P.S. You may enjoy the enclosed, which I happened to see in the correspondence column of a popular gardening paper.

Enclosure:

GOLDEN BELLS. *I should be obliged if you could tell me the name of this pretty yellow flower which we have found in the garden of our new house. We have never seen it before.* R.C.M., Ealing.

—Your shrub is *Forsythia intermedia* var. *spectabilis*. We are surprised that you have never seen it before, as it is now grown in many gardens. The dainty blossoms are produced in profusion in March and April. Its English name is 'golden bells'.

A happy Easter to you! and greetings from Portugal where, on a most sudden impulse, I'm spending ten days. I felt I *must* make the effort to uproot myself; I'd realized that by settling in the country I risked turning from an animal into a vegetable, but I'm now in real danger of becoming a mineral. Yet I can't bear to be away longer when so much is happening in the garden. Cedric Morris has told me where to go and what to look for in Portugal, and I'm following his advice.

I've never been here before, and it's lovely; in a new country, every wayside weed is an excitement—a cousin of something known at home. I've collected several kinds of cistus and various narcissi and other trifles—but nothing rare; for if I call myself a plant-collector you mustn't misunderstand me: I'm not claiming to be another George Forrest or Kingdon Ward. All I mean is that when I go abroad I like to bring back a few plants.

Once Betty and I used to hide them in our sponge-bags or tuck them in my slippers. Then I discovered what ought to be much more widely known—that any-one can get a permit from the Ministry of Agriculture, Fisheries and Food (telegrams: Agrififood London Telex) to import a small parcel of plants for his own garden. They have to be wild flowers, and there's a short black-list. (For example, one may not bring back elm trees, nor plants found growing within a distance of 2 kilometres of any place where wart disease has occurred during the last ten years). As a safeguard against the introduction of disease, the permit is valueless. Naturally the Customs' officials know nothing about foreign wild flowers, and though the Ministry claims the right to inspect the plants—and in our case once did, several months after the bulbs had been planted—such an inspection is simply a waste of public money. However, that's not my affair—or not more so, at least, than wastage of public money in general.

I should say at once that we weren't at all good at bringing plants back, and a lot of them always died in transit. Or subsequently—for the fact is that I'm a terribly incompetent gardener: as Delia once said, 'Darling! the trouble with you is that you've no sense of humus'. But enough survived to make it worth while, and some of these I've moved to Orchards from Hampstead. They remind me of pleasant holidays abroad, and a few of them have literary or historical associations as well. There are little irises from near Daudet's Mill in Provence, primulas from the Brenner, St. Bernard's lilies from the Swiss mountains, tulips from the Pont du Gard, white asphodels from Italy, and pinks from all over the place. And from Bavaria I have the very iris that Dürer drew—I treasure that because it was Jonathan who found it.

And here is one—a periwinkle: you can have a bit of it if you like—that has literary associations. (And for me, sentimental ones too: we collected it on our honeymoon). Do you remember, in Rousseau's *Confessions*, the description of his first arrival with his beloved

'Maman' at Les Charmettes, near Chambéry? On their way up to the house, Maman saw something blue in the hedge and said 'Look! there are some periwinkles still in flower.' Nearly thirty years passed before he saw a periwinkle again—and when he did, the memory of that earlier day came vividly back to him. Well, Mme de Warens and Rousseau saw those periwinkles in 1736, and mine were brought back from that same hedgerow exactly two hundred years later. It's a very ordinary little periwinkle, but I'm glad to have it all the same.

This taste for 'association' plants I presumably 'inherit' from my godfather (just as *you* 'inherit' your interest in flowers from *me*). When he was Chaplain one summer in Bad Nauheim, long before the First World War, he collected an apple-core thrown down by the Kaiser, planted the pips when he got back to England, and so established in West Sussex a little orchard (producing totally inedible apples), which was very properly uprooted by patriots in 1916.

But back to Portugal. The whole country—or such parts of it as I've seen—is one continuous *maquis*, and the cistuses are splendid. So too is the architecture—Batalha in particular: the most magnificent agglomeration of Gothic, pure and impure, that you could possibly imagine. But the language is hopeless, and for inability to make myself understood I was involved in quite an ugly situation here in Tomár yesterday. I must tell you about it.

In a first-floor window-box at a very frequented

L

street corner with market stalls, I noticed a most remarkable carnation with serrated leaves. I stared at it, wondering how I could come by a cutting. A crowd collected and stared where I was staring; I pointed at the window and made vague vegetable gestures which weren't understood. Then the window opened, a very pretty girl looked out, saw me and shut it again with a bang. The crowd decided I was molesting her and became so hostile that I had to retreat.

After some searching I found, in a café, a man who spoke English and who drew up for me in Portuguese a statement explaining what I wanted. Armed with this and a box of caramels I returned to the attack. I was coldly received until the document had been read and passed round; then everyone was eager to help. The girl was summoned, and, because of my ignorance of the word for 'enough', she had half stripped her window-box before I could stop her. Then the caramels were presented, refused, proffered again, accepted. Much hand-shaking all round. 'Long live England!' 'Long live Portugal!' I only hope the cuttings will strike.

I expect to go to Coimbra tomorrow for several days, and then to fly back from Lisbon.

P.S. I brought some Darwin with me to read in the evenings. The following rather pleased me: 'If all the offspring of a spotted Orchis were to survive, the grandchildren of a single plant would nearly clothe, with one uniform green carpet, the entire surface of the land throughout the globe.'

April 23rd

I got back safely from Portugal last week, after a glorious ten days. Glad my letter from Tomár arrived all right; I couldn't find out the Portuguese for Scotland!

I find that while I was away Delia and Humphrey have been to Haarlem for the week-end to see the bulb-fields; I'd warned them not to, having once been caught myself. It seems that first they flew over the tulip-fields —in a fog. Then they were carried a very long way in a stiflingly hot coach with twenty-three Dutchmen smoking large cigars and three English spinsters wishing they weren't. The windows were tight shut and misted over, and when they got to their destination it was raining so hard that they never even got out. They just saw the vague shapes of gigantic red and yellow and purple blankets.

Yet how exciting is *a* tulip, how fascinating the flower's history and geography! First the wild tulips: the greeny-yellow *sylvestris* that is probably a true Britisher; the dapper *clusiana* of the Mediterranean vineyards which Vita Sackville-West compares to little red-and-white soldiers; the great flaming tulips which take the golden road to Samarkand; and a hundred others. Then, in the sixteenth century, the introduction from Turkey into western Europe of the first 'garden' tulip and its meteoric rise to fame—or rather, notoriety. The mad Tulipomania in Holland and elsewhere in the 1620s, when speculators exchanged coaches and even houses for a single bulb. Dumas and his *tulipe noire*. The tulip fêtes in eighteenth-century Turkey, where more than thirteen hundred varieties were displayed, lit by candles—'one to every fourth flower'—placed in the beds. Tom Storer, the Derby engine-driver, who in Victorian England grew prize tulips beside the railway line. The boiled-egg-shaped Darwin tulips and the graceful lily-flowering kinds . . . I could—but I won't —go on for ever!

Your mother wanted to see the Duke of Middlesex's garden at Chipstone, which is open this month under the National Gardens Scheme; so she's just been here for a couple of nights and I drove her over there with Delia and the Admiral. Of course Delia thought your mother 'perfectly *sweet*, and *so* beautiful', and your mother thought Delia had 'such a kind face'. However, they didn't quite 'fuse' as I'd hoped, though there's no better catalyst than the Admiral on such an occasion.

The word 'jealousy' seems a ridiculous one to use in this context, and yet I felt that something not very far removed from it was in the air. The more one sees of women, the more incomprehensible they become.

The gardens (Capability Brown) are very magnificent but rather impersonal: great trees, great lake, great stream, great bridge over great stream, and so on. No *love* anywhere. The Duke is said to be interested, up to a point, in shrubs; the Duchess isn't interested at all. There are far too many rhododendrons for my taste. We also saw the house—very 'stately homes', with signed photographs of royalty everywhere and slick modern portraits of the family that looked pretty silly beside the Gainsboroughs. The ducal pair were either away or very thoroughly hidden.

I really oughtn't to tell you this, but it made Delia laugh and so I'll risk it. Susanna was at Chipstone last week, and discovered that for a further half-crown one could see the Duchess's bedroom and boudoir; her expression was that the Duchess's 'private parts' were well worth the extra money!

They were. The bedroom had been decorated with mythological paintings by a young Greek genius discovered by the Duchess while cruising with Onassis. Some of the scenes were rather *too* Lady Chatterley for your mother, who 'didn't know what things were coming to nowadays'. (It's rather surprising, isn't it, how little she's moved with the times? After all, she's six or seven years younger than I am.) Delia said to me, 'Darling, I couldn't sleep a wink in that bed—could you?' The bed-head (if that's the right word) was painted with a Triton seducing a nymph, egged on by a flight of stucco cupids. I was inclined to agree with her.

Your mother went over with Delia to the window and remarked how fine the great lawn looked, stretching down to the great lake and framed by splendid trees. The Admiral, who had been studying a Leda and Swan through his monocle, joined them and eyed the trees covetously. Delia said, 'Darling, I suppose you're simply *longing* to cut them all down.'

I posted Ruskin's *Proserpina* to you today. You may like to compare this passage—D. H. Lawrence on *Anemone fulgens*—with Ruskin on the corn poppy. It might almost have been written by Ruskin, don't you think? There are some lovely descriptions of flowers scattered through Lawrence's novels, and of course there are also the flower poems. Somewhere—I thought it was in *Sons and Lovers*, but I can't find it—is a splendid bit about daffodils. Here is his anemone:

> If you are passing in the sun, a sudden scarlet faces on to the air, one of the loveliest scarlet apparitions in the world. The inner surface of the Adonis-blood anemone is as fine as velvet, and yet there is no suggestion of pile, not as much as on a velvet rose. And from this inner smoothness issues the red colour, perfectly pure and unknown on earth, no earthiness, and yet solid, not transparent. How a colour manages to be perfectly strong and impervious, yet of a purity that suggests condensed light, yet not luminous, at least, not transparent, is a problem. The poppy in her

radiance is translucent, and the tulip in her utter redness had a touch of opaque earth. But the Adonis-blood anemone is neither translucent nor opaque. It is just pure condensed red, of a velvetiness without velvet, and a scarlet without glow.

In a field behind the Post Office I noticed a few cowslips, and having picked one I started to think about the meaning of the word. 'Bright day's eyes, and the lips of cows,' wrote Ben Jonson. But *are* the flowers particularly like cows' lips? I couldn't see it. I consulted Henry Phillips's *Flora Historica* (1824), but wasn't much impressed by his suggestion that they might be so called 'from the resemblance which their perfume has to the breath of a cow'. So I tried a dictionary: it's not 'cow's-lip' but 'cow-slip'—*slyppe* (or *sloppe*) meaning 'the sloppy droppings of a cow'. How very unromantic!

By the way, do you know if there is anything to be done about naturalized daffodils that have given up flowering? The books always advise dividing the clumps, but my experience is that this only leads to three or four blind bulbs for ever more.

I'm sending you a mixed collection of small flowers from the garden and I hope that at least some of them will reach you alive. The various miniature daffodils ought to open in water. Glorious sunny weather here and the garden is really beginning to look rather nice. At long last the sundial is installed on the terrace, and I think it's a success. I'm so glad you too have been able to sit out-of-doors; I can never quite bring myself to believe that it can be warm in Scotland!

April 28th

When Mrs. Benham called me last Sunday she announced that Susanna was waiting for me but wouldn't give a message. I supposed some major calamity had occurred, dressed hurriedly and stumbled, still half asleep, into the hall. Before I realized what was happening, Susanna flung her arms round my neck, kissed me on both cheeks, thrust a red hard-boiled egg into my hand and said, 'Christ is risen!—it's an old Armenian custom.'

I'd been too startled to resist, too dazed even to remember that we'd had our Easter already; Susanna hadn't shaved and it had been an unnerving experience. 'And now,' she said, '*you* must give *me* an egg'. I told her I hadn't got one; I could smell it was sausages for breakfast. 'Then you must give me back mine,' she told me.

This I gladly did, informing her that Christ had risen but rejecting her proffered cheek. She went on her way to Delia, to whom, as soon as I had sufficiently recovered, I telephoned a warning. But Delia said, 'Darling! *I* should have warned *you*—only I never know when Orthodox Easter is. This happens every year, and Humphrey locks himself up in our bedroom and pretends he's ill. There's the door-bell now. That crashing noise is Humphrey falling upstairs . . .'

Do you realize that, besides being Orthodox Easter, today is also *your* festival—the opening of the 'Floralia'? It seems, curiously enough, to have been one of the most licentious of all the Roman festivals—six days of uninterrupted orgies; one would have thought that anything associated with Flora would have been the height of propriety. Your mother would never have given you that name if she'd read Martial, i, 3 or Seneca Ep., 96!

I'm glad you like the Ruskin book and the bit of D. H. Lawrence. Then of course there's the fascinating and exasperating Reginald Farrer. His great work, *The English Rock-Garden*, is full of powerful passages and is a tremendous achievement. But Farrer could be incredibly silly at times—as when he venomously attacked Ruskin for coining plant-names. For examples of these 'Wardour Street conceits' and 'regrettable brummagem mediaevalisms' he mentions 'Rockfoil' (saxifrage) and 'Bell-flower' (campanula), both sensible names and the latter—which he calls a gratuitous and silly affectation —to be found in the 1597 edition of Gerard's *Herball*.

Farrer writes even more self-consciously than Ruskin and is quite unable to resist the purple ink. Here (for I can't face sending those two bulky volumes)—here he is on *Eritrichium nanum*:

Of [Eritrichium] there is no need to speak, to those

who have seen it; no profit, but vain temptation only, in speaking of it to those who have not. For no eye of faith is quite keen enough to gulp the whole glory of the King of the Alps, as you see those irresistible wads of silky silver nestling into the highest darkest ridges of the granite, and almost hidden from view by the mass of rounded yellow-eyed little faces of a blue so pure and clear and placidly celestial that the richest Forget-me-not by their side takes on a shrill and vulgar note. The blue of Eritrichium is absolute; lacking the tinny violence of *Gentiana verna*'s sapphire satin, and the almost vicious intensity of *Scilla bifolia*, it has a quality of bland and assured perfection impossible to describe as to imagine. And still more impossible to believe by those who have only seen the comparatively rare and squalid stars of faded turquoise which are all that Eritrichium usually condescends to show in cultivation. . . .

Incidentally, it's odd (but *so* typical) of Farrer to devote two thousand words, in a book on the *English* rock-garden, to the description of a plant which he himself admits is indescribable and not worth growing in England. He seems to have attached some kind of a mystique to eritrichium, and it's thanks to him that it's become the plantsman's edelweiss. It has all the qualities of a plantsman's plant: it's rare (except very locally), inaccessible, almost impossible to buy, almost impossible to grow, and not worth growing when you get it. There's a still rarer white form; I wonder if Eric has it.

Since the chief charm of the plant is its blue, I expect that the white form is tremendously sought after by plantsmen.

Have you ever seen eritrichium in the wild? I found it once, on the Col de Clapier. I admit that it's a very good blue. But a large part of its glamour comes from its inaccessibility, from the euphoria which its capture therefore induces, and from Farrer's intensive advertising campaign. The blue of some of the gentians is more startling—that, for example, of Farrer's own gentian, of which he writes, 'In no other plant, except perhaps, *Ipomoea Learii*, or Nemophila, do I know such a shattering acuteness of colour: it is like a clear sky soon after sunrise, shrill and translucent, as if it had a light inside. It literally burns in the alpine turf like an electric jewel, an incandescent turquoise.'

In fact, at times Farrer wrote like the promoter of a new spectacular film, words failing him to convey that it's bigger, better, brighter, bluer, or whatever it may be, than all that's gone before.

I'm so very sorry to hear that your father isn't well. Your mother sounds rather worried about him.

Ever your very affectionate godfather

Wilfrid Sharp

MAY

May 7th

My dearest Flora,

I wish I didn't dislike Mrs. Puttenham so much. I try to remember—and to persuade myself to believe—Helen's story about Mrs. Wishart—but even then . . . She asked me to lunch again—to show off her wealth in general and her garden in particular. There were half-a-dozen other guests, all pretty dull, and Oliver was away in Ireland.

After lunch we were 'shown the garden', which I must admit was looking very good. Then Mrs. Puttenham noticed a rose-bed that hadn't been weeded. A garden-boy was sent to fetch Chandler, to whom she was unnecessarily offensive in front of us all.

I asked her whether she was thinking of sending Oliver to another school 'where the food was better', or was he going to continue with the Rector. She said she hadn't decided, and changed the subject. I've got the feeling that she doesn't like Oliver working in my garden, and if she knows that Chandler has been round here with him she'll dislike that even more.

You ask for my views about arranging flowers: here they are. Let's start with the great set flower-piece that greets you as you enter a Mayfair hotel: 1 doz. sprays of white lilac (stripped), 1 doz. purple ditto, ½ doz. arum lilies, etc., etc., and greenery to taste. No—I don't *dis*like it, but I wouldn't get much diminished pleasure if the whole lot were artificial.

The set-pieces arranged by Chandler for Mrs. Puttenham have a bit more character because the flowers aren't bought by the dozen and aren't uniform. But Chandler aims at what an enthusiast for Japanese flower arrangements has called 'the barbaric massing of colours that constitutes the whole of this art in the West'. In getting his result he isn't in the least interested in the individual flower or the way it grows. When he's in his greenhouse, or mine, he really *looks* at flowers; but as soon as he takes them to a vase they become nothing more than jug-fodder: just blobs of colour to be coaxed into a particular position and bullied into staying there.

Obviously if you're going to use flowers decoratively in a big room you've got to see that they give a big effect. But on the writing-table, the mantelpiece or the window-ledge you can have something intimate; and if you find on the writing-table no little bunch lovingly picked and lovingly arranged by the lady of the house, you can be pretty sure that that woman doesn't really care for flowers at all. She 'has' flowers as she 'has' pictures and books—not because she looks at them or reads them, but because people 'have' them; or, as Ruskin put it, 'many . . . like a fair service of flowers in the greenhouse, as a fair service of plate on the table'. Mrs. Puttenham would no more think of picking a few flowers to put on her writing-table than she would think of washing up the tea things; these are 'jobs for the servants'.

As for those intimate bunches—well, my own preference is for using a tumbler or something quite simple, and I prefer clear glass because I like seeing the stems. Also I like flowers uncrowded—just three or four roses, or a few pinks, or a single spray of columbine. At this very moment I've got on my table beside me a glass vase about eight inches high, with a couple of irises in it and two or three leaves. People seem to imagine that because German irises and carnations and so on have long stems, you've got to have an enormous jugful of them. This is totally unnecessary. But unless you've got a hundred carnations, it's much better to cut them short.

The Chinese and Japanese have of course always understood how important restraint is in flower decoration, and how one should let the individual flower and its growth tell. (Thanks to Mrs. Wycherley all Dewbury now knows this.) But to my mind they've bedevilled the whole thing by a perfectly absurd collection of rules and schools. Basil Chamberlain says in his *Things Japanese* that 'sober enquiry into botanical fact' produces 'no warrant for the hard-and-fast set of linear rules elaborated by a coterie of dilettanti in the fifteenth century'; and I couldn't agree more. If you want some idea of how ridiculously complex and hieratic it is, I'll lend you Sadler's book.

I see that in the most up-to-date work on the subject
—Norman Sparnon's *Japanese Flower Arrangement,
Classical and Modern*—some of the highly-commended
set-pieces are made without using flowers at all—just
wire and so on, bent into forms that suggest organic
growth. Surely this is *reductio ad absurdum*!

I do wish you could see my garden now; it's really
looking rather good. The lilacs are splendid this year.
So are the Judas trees, choisyas and wisterias, *Viburnum
carlesii*, the single kerrias, and various sorts of prunus,
malus and broom. I've photographed the davidia (which
your mother *will* call 'a *rather* unique' tree) and am
sending a print to the *Gardeners Chronicle*. All these
plants survived Trotter's lustrum of misrule, during
which much was doubtless lost. The terrace is tubbed
with wallflowers which deluge me with smell as I write
this in the loggia.

You say you'd like to go plant-collecting in China
one day? Well—think twice; for this is the kind of thing
that might happen to you:

> At the end of eight days I had ceased to care whether
> I lived or died—my feet swollen out of all shape, my
> hands and face torn with thorns, and my whole
> person caked with mire. I was nearly dead through
> hunger and fatigue, and . . . quite delirious for a time.
> Then I knew that the end was near, and determined
> to make one more bid for life. . . .

That was George Forrest in Yunnan in 1895, yet
luckier than the rest of his party of eighty, most of

whom were killed outright or tortured to death by lamas. Think of Père Soulié, who gave you the common purple buddleia—tortured for twelve days by Tibetan monks and finally shot; of his collaborator, Bourdonnec, who was wounded by poisoned arrows and then beheaded; and of their successor, Monbeig, also murdered. Think of Robert Fortune three times attacked by river pirates, of Frank Meyer drowned in the Yangtse, of Wilson overwhelmed by a landslide and permanently lamed soon after getting *Lilium regale* for you. That's what people suffered so that you could have a few pretty flowers in your garden; and I sometimes think that it might be a nice gesture to use black-edged labels for plants whose introducers came to untimely ends in their pursuit. It would at least remind us of our debt.

Or would you like to go even further afield and try the Pacific Islands? Then read the horrifying story of how David Douglas was gored to death in the Sandwich Islands when he fell into a pit made to catch wild bulls.

Do you still want to go?

Yet perhaps, when you read of the thrill of discovery of an important new plant, you still may. Here is part of Wilson's account, in the highly-perfumed prose beloved of plant-collectors, of his finding of his lily in western China (Szechwan) in 1903:

There in narrow, semi-arid valleys, down which thunder torrents, and encompassed by mountains composed of mud-shales and granites, whose peaks are clothed with eternal snow, the Regal Lily has its home. In summer the heat is terrific, in winter the cold is intense, and at all seasons these valleys are subject to sudden and violent windstorms against which neither man nor beast can make headway. There, in June, by the wayside, in rock-crevices by the torrent's edge, and high up on the mountainside and precipice, this Lily in full bloom greets the weary traveller. Not in twos or threes but in hundreds, in thousands, aye, in tens of thousands.

Aye—in millions, no doubt. Then Wilson describes the flower, 'more or less wine-coloured without, pure white and lustrous in the face, clear canary-yellow within the tube and each stamen filament tipped with a golden anther'. He writes of the cool morning and evening air 'laden with delicious perfume', and the lonely, semi-desert region transformed for a brief season 'into a veritable fairyland'. Perhaps it's worth while after all!

In any case, there are dangers enough for the stay-at-home gardener: the fall from a ladder, a garden fork through the foot, lockjaw from a neglected scratch, lumbago, strained muscles . . . Or worse: do you know the tragic story, told in John Cowell's *The Curious and Profitable Gardener* (1730), of his flowering of the great American aloe, *Agave americana?*

It had been flowered in England before; but it was still a considerable rarity, and Cowell's specimen in his

M

Hoxton nursery gardens was a magnificent plant, believed to be more than 70 years old. As the flower spike grew, at the rate of six or seven inches a day, Cowell gradually increased the height of the tower he had built to shelter it—a tower which had glass on the south side only. Then he waited for the bang—because a French author had written that in France the opening of the flowers 'faisait un grand bruit . . .' ('created a great stir . . .'), and Cowell had been given to understand that this meant that they would explode like the firing of a cannon.

In due course the first flower opened—splendidly but silently—and crowds flocked to the gardens, and paid handsomely, to see the vegetable giant. Now comes the sad part of the story, and I'll give it you in Cowell's own words. One day among the throng of visitors there appeared three Men habited like Gentlemen . . .

who no sooner were come to the Plant, but one of them began to break off the Buds; and being desired to desist, took hold of the main Stem, and endeavour'd to break it by violence; but it was luckily, much too strong to give way to their base Intent. This their attempt was soon discover'd by all the Gentlemen and Ladies in my Garden, and I was call'd to the Assistance of my Servant, and to save my Plant from the fury of their Rage: When immediately one, who was on the top of the Stair-case in my Aloe-House, being intreated by me to come down, fell a swearing, and drew his Sword upon my Man, telling him he would run him through the Body if he offer'd to assist me; and in the mean time kick'd me on the Head while I offer'd to go up, while another at the bottom of the Stairs, one of his Companions, pull'd me by the Legs; and a third of them wounded me with his Sword in two places of my Neck, so that I was under the Surgeon's hands many Weeks, devoid of attending the curious Persons that did me the honour of coming to my Garden . . .

Poor Cowell!—he had thus lost 'the fairest Prospect of possessing an easy Fortune for my Life'. Worse still—he feared he might have 'disobliged' the nobility who patronized his nursery garden.

And here are Humphrey and Delia, just arriving for a drink. Delia is always asking after you, and if you've got the energy I'm sure she'd like a letter. It would be a good investment because you'd get a glorious one back.

P.S. So you were named after *St.* Flora! Well—that's the first I've heard of it. I see from Butler's *Lives of the Saints* that there were three of them—two virgin-martyrs and St. Brigid's Irish cook. Which is yours?

A heavy storm has battered everyone's tulips to the ground, and Delia tells me that cute little Christine Peters has thrilled the village by announcing, 'Look, Mummy! All the tulips are *saying their prayers*!' She is an odious child—precocious, bumptious, and horribly spoilt by Helen who thinks she's a genius.

May 14th

Much though I shall regret not seeing you again for a while, I think you are very wise to stay on in Edinburgh. Obviously the physiotherapy treatment the hospital is giving you is doing so much good. And with your father ill, I really believe it would be too much for your mother to have you at home at present. It was a triumph getting to the theatre; how kind of Mr. McGrath to take you.

Curiously enough, just after I'd written to you about plant-collectors there arrived for me, from my friend Dr. Schultes of Harvard, a handful of pamphlets dealing with his twenty years of field-work in the Colombian Amazon and elsewhere in southern and central America. Fascinating stuff about his discovery of new drug plants and investigation of native narcotics, a number of which he bravely sampled. Worship of sacred narcotic mushrooms by the Mayas, who made stone images of them three thousand years ago. And strangest fact of all: the aborigines of British Guiana are tobacco addicts, but they prefer to take it *in the form of an enema*! *A chacun son goût.*

I took, as I always do, a book (Ruskin) to read over my solitary dinner last night; but Mrs. Benham had put so charming a posy on my dining-table that for a time I got no reading done. A few primroses and grape hyacinths, a wild anemone or two (var. *Robinsoniana*, with silvery-blue flowers), a sprig of wallflower, a little tulip which I can't identify, a couple of pheasant's eye narcissi, a spray of that blue flower that isn't forget-me-not (but I *have* forgot), one piece of honesty, a pulsatilla and a yellow auricula that I brought back from the Dolomites in the forties. Five or six distinct smells, the auricula easily winning; is there any other flower that smells so deliciously of spring?

Then I opened my Ruskin (at random) and read, 'Much revived and pleased by a crimson convolvulus and three nasturtiums on my white breakfast-table. I never saw before what a wonderful thing a nasturtium was, in the set of it on the stalk.' A curious coincidence!

How right, incidentally, Ruskin is about the nasturtium—loveliest of Peruvian flowers. And personally I like its smell. Parkinson (who grew the smaller kind) did too, and recommended mixing carnations and nasturtiums 'to make a Delicate Tussimussie or Nose-gay'.

Nasturtium means 'nose-twister' (try biting a leaf!); but our garden nasturtium is, of course, botanically Tropaeolum—a word connected with *tropaeum*, a trophy. Linnaeus coined it because the nasturtium's rounded leaves reminded him of shields and its flowers of 'spear-pierced blood-stained golden helmets'. Linnaeus's daughter, Elizabeth Christina, alleged that she saw nasturtium flowers emit periodic sparks 'as of an electrical kind' at dusk; and so did Goethe. 'Singular leaves, fire-coloured flowers, a lady, sparks of light, and an evening—what might not a poet make of all these?' asks the author of *Flora Domestica*. So far as I know, the poets have made nothing of them; and as for the botanists, they seem to be agreed that Miss Linnaeus and Goethe were 'seeing things'.

You ask me to describe Mrs. Puttenham's appearance. It's not necessary. You know Rubens' 'Rape of the Sabines' in the National Gallery? Well, Mrs. P. is the central Sabine—the one with clasped hands and an expression of rather token resistance.

And if Mrs. Puttenham is a Rubens, then Lord Pheen is a Greco—one of the mourners at Count Orgaz' funeral: sixty, sallow, black hair and neatly trimmed beard both greying. He is one of those Irish peers of whom no one is aware until their obituaries appear in *The Times*, and he lives in almost monastic seclusion among his flowers. I'd met him once and very briefly at Eric's, and liked what I saw of him; but he was a plantsman, and I thought that one Eric was enough. However, when he sent me a very friendly invitation to come and see some things he'd brought back a year or two ago from the Lebanon, I accepted.

And how glad I am that I did! To watch Lord Pheen with his flowers is more than a pleasure: it's an education. He really *loves* his plants. Eric bullies and frightens his plants into flowering; Pheen coaxes and caresses them. I wish you could have seen him in his greenhouse, picking up a little pot of fritillaries as tenderly as a connoisseur handling a piece of eggshell porcelain. He's collected plants from all over the world, and every one of them has its memories and associations. 'That iris,' he said, 'cost me a broken wrist, but it was almost worth it. I suppose *susiana* is rather a foolish name for it—it's never been found in Persia; but I like the sound of it all the same. Look at the texture of the petals through this lens. Gerard says it's like a guinea-fowl, and I think Parkinson compares it to a snake's skin. Oh, and Dykes —he said it looked like a piece of newspaper on which the ink had run: which is unkind. I've tried again and again to paint it, but I can't get it at all.

'I expect you know that Busbecq sent it back from Constantinople about four hundred years ago. He'd gone there from Vienna as Ambassador to Suleiman the Magnificent. You haven't read Busbecq's Letters? Then you must let me lend them you; they're delightful. He was a keen gardener, and something of a zoologist too. He sent back lilacs and other shrubs and trees and, of course, the first garden tulips. Gerard's name for this iris was the Turkey Flower-de-Luce. He says something about the falls being like "gaping hoods"; rather

a good description of them, don't you think? He also
—if I remember rightly—says it "prospered" in his
London garden. It doesn't prosper in most English
gardens today, although I dare say some of the other
irises in that group are even harder. Round did a
very nice drawing of it for Dykes's Iris book; the
picture in the Botanical Magazine doesn't do it jus-
tice.'

He'll talk like that about any flower you care to mention. His knowledge is incredible; and of course he has
a splendid library, which he has told me I can use. He
never flourishes Latin names in your face, but he knows
them all if you ask him. I said that he *looked* Spanish,
but in character he's more like those Chinese philos-
ophers who withdraw from the world and live in solitude
and in harmony with Nature.

When I came to leave, he gave me a handful of
tigridia bulbs. 'They're fantastic things,' he said—'so
fantastic that when Gerard was shown a drawing of one
he scornfully dismissed it as "meere fiction". It's not
too late to plant them now. They always remind me of a
trip I made to Central America twenty years ago. Many
people know that tigridias come from Blom's; so few
seem to know, or to care, that they also come from
Mexico.'

I discovered that Delia hadn't met Pheen (who does
in fact live some way off), so I immediately asked them
both to lunch. I suspect that Pheen, who is a staunch
bachelor, has rather a low opinion of women in general,
but, as I hoped, he took to Delia instantly. And Delia

thought him '*absolutely* sweet'—so the party was a great success. We went over to Wisley afterwards, and Delia was astonished at his display of knowledge—no, 'display' is quite the wrong word: Pheen never 'shows off'; the facts are just *there*, and the right question draws them out.

Pheen had given some bulbs to Wisley, and we went to look at them in those greenhouses and frames marked 'private' near the alpine house. There was a lovely little green and maroon fritillary that he'd found in Turkey, and apparently it's a new species. Delia said, 'I *do* hope they call it *Pheenii*.' Pheen said, 'Not if *I* have anything to do with it.'

Some of Susanna's tulips are now out, some over, others just opening—and it would seem that they aren't all Armenian. The coppery one is obviously *Hageri*, which I always think a bit dull. Another might be *Whittallii*, usually found in Anatolia. There is a superb deep crimson which I covet and which could be *armena*, and a dazzling scarlet that is certainly *linifolia*. Others I can't place: could it be *Sprengeri* that's just about to open? I know it's one of the latest to flower. Are you good on tulips?

Anyhow, Susanna doesn't want to know their names. To her these tulips are the symbols of her homeland, and ought, she feels, if named they must be, to commemorate her own towns or her own countrymen. 'How would you wish your buttercups to be called *Tumaniantzii*?' she asked me. 'I don't want my tulips called after Mr. Whittall. Who was this Whittall?' 'He lived in Smyrna,' I told her. 'I suppose he was a consul or a merchant—I don't know which—and wandered about Asia Minor digging up your tulips and sending them to England.' 'And if I wander about England and send your buttercups to Mush—how then?'

I said I was afraid she'd left it too late. But she has my sympathy, just as the Spaniards have who want Gibraltar back and ask how *we* would like it if they owned Portland Bill. However, I rather think it may now take a lot of diplomacy and buns before I get any of those crimson tulips that I've set my heart on.

But for the moment we've lost our Lily (Susanna = Lily). She left yesterday for Italy for six weeks—her first visit. There have been tremendous preparations: constant calls to borrow books and to return books (if not meanwhile lost), to consult maps, to ask advice of every kind. She's gone alone, and the principal advice I gave her was that she simply *must* pull herself together and *not* lose anything vital; should she become parted from her money or her passport she might find herself in quite an awkward fix, especially since she isn't a British subject. I breathed a relieved sigh when she finally departed, and so did Oliver who has been helping me again in the garden; heaven knows what a mishmash of information and misinformation she'll deluge me with when she gets back.

However, I do believe that she has now accepted the fact that her chances of becoming the second Mrs. Sharp are so slender as to be negligible. For this at least I am thankful.

P.S. By the way—I quite forgot to tell you that poor Delia has had a burglar. However, he took the Victorian silver and left the Georgian, so it might have been worse.

May 21st

Dinner with the Stringers, to meet their daughter and son-in-law, Averil and Henry Barton, who are staying the week-end with them. Henry is a lawyer, and singularly unattractive; Averil I liked. The Rector and his daughter Daphne were there too—an odd choice, since Henry turned out to be a militant agnostic—and they had brought with them a young Australian called Adams, who was very obviously courting Daphne. I suspect that Stringer wanted to let off steam about the Church of England and thought Henry would be a useful ally. I don't quite know what my function was; perhaps just to be at the receiving end of Mrs. Stringer's platitudes. It was a disastrous and embarrassing evening.

Over the soup (Knorr's tomato) Stringer delivered a

lecture on the subject of the revision of the Prayer Book, which he wanted entirely rewritten—doubtless by himself. Usher, who's a scholar, was against tampering with the language in any way. Henry said, ' "Give us this day our daily Energen roll and vitamin pill"— that's what we mean; then why not say it?' I refused to join in, and made futile conversation with Mrs. Stringer, who thought we didn't look like getting any summer this year, could never remember a wetter March, and so on. Daphne, sitting on my right, agreed; she really is extraordinarily pretty, but it's the kind of prettiness that depends almost entirely upon the bloom of youth, and when that's gone there'll be little left. The Australian gazed at her and barely uttered.

With half an ear I heard Henry saying, 'I expect you know the story of the bishop who tried to buy a small crucifix at a W. H. Smith's somewhere in the provinces. "No, Sir," said the girl behind the counter. "We don t stock it. Most people nowadays prefer Durofix".' Averil, too cut off to join in our conversation about the relative merits of Bude and Torquay for a summer holiday ('If we *do* get any summer this year'), sat in silence.

Suddenly I realized that Mrs. Stringer's flow of platitudes was nothing but a cloak to her abject misery and embarrassment. Then she saw that I understood, and 'her countenance quickly graduated' (as Thomas Hardy puts it somewhere) 'from Maiden's Blush, through all the varieties of the Provence down to the Crimson Tuscany'. At last I could bear it no longer. When

Henry paused a moment for breath I broke off in the middle of a remark to Mrs. Stringer and asked the Colonel how his gladioli were coming along: they're his favourite flower. Stringer abandoned religion and immediately embarked upon a lecture on the only right way to treat bulbs, corms and tubers. The Rector and Mrs. Stringer both made me almost imperceptible gestures of gratitude.

At ten o'clock the Rector rose to go, so I took the chance to escape. Stringer said, 'The night is still young. Don't go running away yet. Have a whisky for the road!' But I was firm. As I walked down the drive with the Rector and his party I couldn't resist expressing my sympathy. Usher smiled wanly and said, 'Yes, my patience was sorely tried.'

I really don't know which is worse: dinner with the Stringers, or dinner with the Moons (followed by paper games, always won by Mrs. Moon who makes up her own rules as she goes along). I couldn't help wondering how it would have turned out if dear Colonel Moon had married Mrs. Stringer, and Colonel Stringer Mrs. Moon. I think the two Moons would have been blissfully happy, and that either Colonel Stringer or his wife would have committed murder or suicide before the end of their honeymoon. I find it absolutely incomprehensible that Delia can find Colonel Stringer attractive.

My whole room is scented by a great pot of Madonna lilies that I've just brought in from the cool greenhouse; I wish you could see it. I absolutely agree with Phoebe Lawrence (can't remember whether you know her or not) that the 'white lily', as it always used to be called, is the best of the lot. Lily experts will hold up their hands in horror at this blasphemy—but I don't care; I've grown a fair number of different kinds in my time and I still think so. *Lilium candidum* has three or four thousand years of history and almost as much of legend behind it, and no modern lily, however 'easy' or free-flowering or enormous or disease-proof or exotic, can usurp its place in my affections. The Madonna lily is to the Regale lily as is the Parthenon to the Mansion House, and, incidentally, it (I mean the Madonna lily) has the best smell of them all—what Evelyn calls 'a cardiaque and most refreshing halitus'. Regale smells like a Bond Street hairdresser's.

It looks as though the Madonna lily's real home is the Balkans. But as a healing plant—it was believed to be a panacea for wounds, severed nerves and serpents' bites—it probably travelled along with the armies of the ancient world and so settled down in places as far apart as Afghanistan and Italy. It's even found in an apparently wild state in the Canary Islands. There's a lovely (though much reconstructed) picture of it painted about 3,500 years ago on a Cretan wall; but it was not until the Christian Church singled it out as a symbol of purity that it became the most painted and most popular of all flowers. Every religious artist of the Renaissance placed it in the hand of the Archangel Gabriel or in a pot at the Virgin's feet. It stands in the green meadow of the van Eycks' great altarpiece at Ghent, and it grew in monastery gardens all over Europe (remind me to

tell you one day about Walafrid Strabo). Netherlands'
artists, like London florists, were supposed to remove
the stamens (and for reasons not so different as you
might imagine), but the former frequently refused to
play.

Besides all these historical and religious associations
I've got some personal ones: of the cottage gardens of
my childhood; of our own herbaceous border at the
Vicarage; of the lily growing apparently wild and in
profusion in the vineyards above Lerici. It's no good;
for me it will always be *the* lily, and Eric Leighton can
have every Oregon hybrid that he likes, ordinary bulbs
of them or 'jumbo size' (as I see large bulbs are now
abominably called in some of the catalogues), so long as
I may grow my Madonna lilies as I wish and walk
beside them in my garden on a warm July evening.

My davidia is still making a fine show. I expect you
know what it looks like, with its great white bracts that
flutter like handkerchiefs; in fact, it's sometimes called
the 'pocket-handkerchief tree'. E. H. Wilson, in his
Aristocrats of the Garden, gives an exciting account of the
expedition he made to China in 1899 to try to find the
single specimen marked down by Dr. Henry eleven
years earlier. After months of difficult travel through
wild country where the natives were in full revolt, he
came at last upon its stump, standing beside the house
that had just been built from its branches!

The following year he explored another remote region where Père David (of 'Père David's deer' fame)
had first found the davidia in 1869. This time he was

lucky. In due course huge quantities of seed were sent back to England where they were 'pre-treated' in various ways—with hot water and cold water, with abrasion, and all the other tricks of the trade. Some were then sown in hot houses, others in cold houses, yet others in the open. For a whole year nothing happened; then suddenly the seeds that had been sown out of doors began to germinate, and soon there were 30,000 plants ready for distribution to the gardeners of England.

My cobaea seedlings are growing so obstreperously that I've been obliged to plant them out against my south wall near the loggia. The moonflowers have been put in a very big pot in the greenhouse. I've not been very successful with morning glories (you'll remember the show they made at Hampstead, but then I used to buy the plants); is it too *much*, or too *little*, water that I give them? I shall never know.

Give (always, please—I never remember) appropriate greetings to your aunt; it's very satisfactory that you get on so well together, and I know, from your mother, how much she enjoys having you.

P.S. A pair of sparrows are building a nest against my loggia. When I come out, they play the innocent: pretend they don't live there at all; butter wouldn't melt in their beaks, and so on. A moment later they repay my hospitality by using the petals of my polyanthus for interior decoration. I don't know about birds, but isn't this rather late in the season for nest-making? Perhaps it's a case of *secondes noces*.

May 31st

If one is going to have flowers 'en masse', then I don't think there's anything better than a field of buttercups (they're glorious this year). Poppies run it close— or perhaps I should say 'ran', because selective weed-killers have almost exterminated them. A bluebell wood? a primrose coppice? A field of fritillaries? It's hard to choose.

But for a mixed bag, nothing in England can touch an alpine meadow in spring, summed up for me since childhood by MacWhirter's 'June in the Austrian Tyrol', painted at Gosau in the Salzkammergut in the early nineties. The flowers are 'clustered for very love', said Edward Cook in his *Popular Handbook to the Tate Gallery*, published in the days when it was still respectable to admire MacWhirter and still permissible to write with fervour. I'm no longer capable of judging whether it's a 'good' or a 'bad' picture; the pleasure I get from it is frankly sentimental (and why not? Why shouldn't I pick up any pleasure that's going?). I won-

N

der whether the Tate Gallery, which is nowadays far too
avant-garde to exhibit it, would lend it me for a year or
two.

But talking of buttercups, have I ever told you the
sad story of the Bournemouth Cricket Week? When I
was about ten, my father took me, as a special treat, to
see Hampshire play—shall we say, Surrey? I don't remember. It seems that there was one of those spectacular
ten-minutes-to-go, six-runs-to-make, one-wicket-to-fall
finishes (sheer Henry Newbolt!), and a great hush fell
over the stands. Then suddenly a cry went up: Hampshire had won. My father turned to share with me the
joys of victory. But—I WAS NOT THERE! Bored stiff by
the whole procedure I had wandered away behind the
stands and was at that very moment returning triumphantly with an enormous armful of buttercups.

Of course everyone was very kind—kind as one is to
an invalid; but I think it was then that my father first
suspected that I would never play for England. Yet I
still believe I was better employed picking buttercups
than watching that dreary game upon which I was later
to have to waste so many hundreds of hours.

What set me thinking about massed flowers was a
visit I paid with Helen to the Savill Gardens in Windsor
Great Park. So much of it is so brilliantly done, and the
view across the lake almost reconciled me to rhododendrons and, what is far more remarkable, momentarily
struck Helen dumb. I really ought to make the effort to
take her on more expeditions of this kind, because
she enjoys them so enormously; but I always come

home with a headache. She's quite incapable of relaxing.

Then we went on to the punch-bowl of Kurume azaleas in the Valley Gardens. . . . It beats the Dutch bulb-
fields into a frazzle (as Susanna would say). The whole
place was stiff with colour-photographers; how strange
that people who very likely distemper the walls of their
rooms mist-green or pale primrose should imagine that
nothing but crude magenta, scarlet and crimson is worth
photographing! I couldn't help thinking how much
cheaper it would have been, in the long run, to have
cemented the whole bowl and sprayed it all the colours
of the rainbow with Paripan. Practically no upkeep.
Colour all the year round . . .

Why, you will ask, do I like poppy-fields and dislike
azalea-bowls? Partly, no doubt, because I like the poppy
family and dislike most rhododendrons; other than that,
I suppose it's just a case of Dr. Fell, where reason plays
no part.

'Re'—as they say—writing about flowers, another
thing to guard against is facetiousness. I confess I
haven't at all a clear conscience in this respect; in the
past I've written stuff that would certainly make me
blush if I were to read it again now. How do you like
this, from W. E. Johns's *The Passing Show*:

Meconopsis integrifolia who must surely have escaped
from the madhouse, with her sunshade inside out, is
leaning against old man primula denticulata whom
somebody has hit in the eye with a lump of mud. Not
far away a rose is crawling about on the ground as

though she had lost something; her perfume, I expect. Well, I did what I could for them all. Just as I had finished I discovered a young Saxifrage apiculata screaming for its mother, so I took him into the alpine house where mamma was busy trying on a new yellow two-piece suit.

The writer of the Foreword says of the author, 'I should say that no one taught him how to write; he did not even teach himself.' Clearly sarcasm is not intended, for he continues, 'He is a born writer . . .'

There are lots of books of this kind—books in which a mouse (called 'Machiavelli') systematically eats its way through the newly-planted crocus corms; where there is trouble with the garden hose, whose jet inevitably catches the next-door neighbour full in the eye; where slugs are enormous in their malevolence and 'Old Man Luck' is always on the side of the garden rabbit ('in my gentian bed of all places, its jaws working ominously!'); where the gardener is called 'Sludge' and all the hydrangeas get hydrophobia. Consider the following (Captain Johns again):

If all the cuckoo-spit in my borders was spat by cuckoos, then there are more cuckoos in the world than I thought there were. They *would* choose *my* garden for the Great Spring Open Expectoration Championship.

Consider it—and take warning.

I got Mrs. Puttenham's (extremely reluctant) permission to take Oliver with me to the Chelsea Flower

Show. He made an agreeable companion; I had expected him to be eager, but I was surprised at his knowledge and—what for a son of Mrs. Puttenham's seemed very improbable—his taste. For example, he knew a roscoea (which I'm sure Chandler doesn't grow) the moment he saw it, and the sort of soil and conditions it needs. As for his taste—when I say he has good taste I merely mean, of course, that it coincides with my own! He'd never been to Chelsea before, and I was completely footsore before I could drag him away. He ordered a number of plants and insisted upon giving me some auriculas that I'd admired, because it had been 'quite the nicest day I've had for a long time.' Moreover, he wasn't rude once. On the way home I couldn't help thinking of Jonathan, and how, if he'd lived, he'd now have been almost exactly Oliver's age. Poor Betty never got over his death. Nor, I suppose, have I.

Delia, whom I met in the village yesterday, said to me, 'Darling! you're coming back to have some sherry with me because I want to show you something *so* extraordinary.' She wouldn't say what it was; but it turned out to be something quite absurd yet really rather charming: a mullein *sitting on a seat*! It had come up through the slats of the seat and then a bird or slug had nipped the stem partly through. So to save over-exerting itself it had worked its way horizontally until it had sufficiently recovered to grow upwards again. It was sitting looking rather prim and self-conscious, but very comfortable, exactly in the middle of the seat, so we sat down each side of it and drank our sherry.

'Darling!' Delia said, 'don't you think it's wonderful that flowers are teetotalers: I mean to get through life without alcohol and yet look so happy and beautiful? But I suppose vines are permanently intoxicated. Look at that bumble bee! Did you know that bumble bees were all spinster aunts who work like blacks to look after their nieces and don't really have any fun at all?'

'I didn't,' I said, 'and I very much doubt it. But did *you* know that some of the Malayan orchids do best when "watered" with beer, that some of the South American ones make bees drunk in order to get them where they want them, and that neat whisky is the best cure for mealy-bug on grapes?' Delia said she did not, and that she very much doubted it.

I'm glad to say that I've been able to be of some use to Delia and Humphrey, though it's a miserably small return for all their kindness. Humphrey consulted me about their investments, and I advised them to sell, just in time, some extremely dubious shares that have since dropped to almost nothing. So there's some advantage in having been in the City. Delia, by the way, has sent her burglar, who is doing three months, a copy of Oman's *English Domestic Silver*; she felt so *terribly* sorry for him, she said, for not knowing which spoons to take.

Ever your very affectionate godfather

Wilfrid Sharp

JUNE

My dearest Flora,

June is here and 'What is one to say about June?' asks dear old Gertrude Jekyll in her *Wood and Garden*. Quite a lot, it turns out, though she has nothing strikingly new to tell of 'the soft cooing of the wood-dove, the glad song of many birds, the flitting of butter-flies, the hum of all the little winged people among the branches, the sweet earth-scents,' and so on. 'June,' she discovers, 'is the time of Roses.' Then she rushes up into her wood and cries aloud for very joy, 'June is here —June is here; thank God for lovely June!' I can't quite bring myself to do this; but in my own simpler, silenter way I'm enjoying the summer, though I could get along with fewer little winged people among my branches.

I must tell you of a lunatic expedition I've just made. The other day Delia said, 'Darling, I want to take you to luncheon—you and Susanna—with May Stillman. She lives in an antiseptic triangular house and she's quite mad. Will you come?' Of course I said I would.

It was miles—somewhere near Maidstone. Delia insisted upon driving us, which I didn't much care for, and on the way Susanna and I were told a bit more about Mrs. Stillman, who had been at St. Paul's with Delia. Her husband was rich—something in the City—and had given May more or less *carte blanche* to indulge in the art of gracious contemporary living. 'I won't tell you the rest,' Delia said. 'You shall see for yourselves. Darling, did you *really* think I was going to hit that van?' 'Yes,' I said. 'Frankly I did.'

May was like a mole, all dressed in mushroom-coloured corduroy and blinking as she emerged from a grove of rubber-plants to greet us. Her black hair was clipped horizontally across the middle of her forehead, like that of a Japanese doll, and she can't have been much more than five feet tall. Her face was circular and as dead white as if it had been chalked. I didn't like her the better for calling Delia 'Diddles'—apparently her nickname at school.

But the house was far odder than May. It really *was* triangular, and mostly made of glass, and the roof sloped at about thirty degrees to the horizontal. It was a bungalow—but rather large, so that the highest line of the roof was about 25 feet, and the lowest corner perhaps six feet, above ground level. Another unusual feature was that none of the walls, interior or exterior, was vertical. Delia whispered to me, 'Darling, I always feel just slightly *seasick* in this room.'

We were then in the main living-room, which was more or less hexagonal and had a glossy black ceiling.

The floor was pebbled and very painful indeed to the feet, and through a vent somewhere among the pebbles rose a trickle of *musique concrète* played on a concealed gramophone. The chairs and tables were all made of glass (I suppose it was really perspex or something) and as triangular as circumstances permitted—which didn't add to the comfort of the chairs. There were two abstract paintings screwed on to the sloping walls, and in one corner of the hexagon stood a sort of barbed-wire entanglement on a glass pedestal. Susanna uttered a cry of joy and rushed towards it.

'The Unknown Political Prisoner,' said May. 'But you oughtn't to look at it yet; your eyes aren't acclimatized to the light. It's by an Armenian sculptor who's working in Paris. There's a little group of them who live together and have everything in common. But perhaps you know them, Miss Tumaniantz?'

Of course it just *made* Susanna's day—not that it really needed more making, because she was already quite bowled over by the intoxicating beauty of everything. Delia and I tried hard to be appreciative; but even when our eyes had become acclimatized there seemed to be little that one could say, and in any case Susanna was doing enough for us all. Then Delia said, 'Darling May, I always think the colour of your walls is *absolute* bliss. Where on earth did you find it?' May explained that the basic colour was called—well, I can't remember what, but something absurd like 'reindeer's breath', and that there was only one firm—'quite a *little* firm'—in Helsinki where you could get it. 'I had the room painted seven times before I got it exactly right,' she added. 'In the end the smallest pinch of umber did it.'

I wondered how Mr. Stillman (he was away) fitted into all this, and made a tentative enquiry. 'Poor Bobby!' May said. 'And I really *have* tried to educate him. You ought to see his study; it would simply horrify you.' I replied that I would very much like to.

We passed down a long and tapering corridor much blocked by two large pieces of modern sculpture, looking like Gruyère cheese, that were ecstatically acclaimed by Susanna. 'Henry Moore and Barbara Hepworth, of course,' May explained. 'Bobby wouldn't have them in the hall: he thought they looked indecent. He's so *terribly* reactionary. I had half a mind to put them in the loos—Henry's in the "gents", of course—and have them plumbed; it would have served Bobby right.'

Mr. Stillman's study was at the six-foot corner of the house. It was a typically Victorian room, with comfortable leather armchairs, Eton and Trinity Cambridge rowing groups, oars, and so on. 'It looks very cosy,' I ventured rashly. May snorted and hurried us away. 'Now let's go and have lunch,' she said. 'I hope you can eat *douchkas*; they really ought to be made with vine leaves, of course, but I always use dock and you can hardly tell the difference. Docks do very well here. Then something *very* special—hot lobster with chocolate sauce: it's an old Bulgarian recipe . . .'

After lunch we walked round the garden. It was hideously neglected, but May 'showed it off' as though it were Wisley. Instinctively I stooped to pull up a weed—(Query: is it a kindness, or merely bad manners, to pull up weeds in other people's gardens?)—but May stopped me: '*Please* don't damage my darling groundsel,' she said. 'And now let's go and look at the ground elder; it's one of my favourites.'

To make conversation, I asked her why her lilacs didn't flower. 'Oh but they *would*,' she said, '*if I let them*! I always get Bobby to cut the buds off as soon as they show. I think its flowers are so *vulgar*, don't you?' I replied that, to be perfectly honest, I rather liked them. She looked pityingly at me, and I think she was probably wondering whether I too had leather armchairs and rowing groups at home. It made me realize, very forcibly, how appallingly bourgeois I was. I only wish your mother had been present.

On the way back, Delia told me something that surprised me more than anything I had seen that day: 'You'd never guess it, Darling, would you, that May used to play lacrosse for Wales?'

Dear old Miss Lawrence is 90 today, so I've been over (with a bunch of the old roses and a bottle of port) to Redhill to see her. I think I've mentioned her name to you. I've known her, and loved her, for years. She's the eldest of three spinster sisters—Phoebe, Emily and Carrie—and they all live, and have always lived, together in an old farmhouse that has been in the family for a couple of centuries.

When they first knew it, it was in the depths of the country; but gradually it has been caught up in the

tentacles of Redhill and Reigate—squashed between the
two towns, is perhaps a more accurate description. First
came a school, its playground abutting their wall, its
footballs bouncing among their lilies and scaring their
tame robin; and because the pert little boys got sweets
when they came round to fetch them, they soon started
kicking them over on purpose.

Then a factory uprose to the north, with two smoke-
belching chimneys and a siren; then a Tudor-style
housing estate hirsute with TV aerials, whose gothic inhabitants blast their wirelesses all day long. As for the
road to the south—well, there's talk of a bypass and a
quarter of their beloved garden being snatched away by
the authorities.

I found Phoebe on her knees, weeding. What she
could find to weed, I really couldn't imagine: it was all
as spotless as a show garden at Chelsea. You know that
I don't really like tidiness as such. But Phoebe's tidiness
isn't due to pettiness, or to any miserable notion that
tidiness is in itself a virtue; she keeps her garden weed-
free because weeds are the potential murderers of her
adored phloxes, pinks, columbines, and so on. For of
course she grows all the old-fashioned flowers (it was
she who gave me those laced pinks I sent you last week)
—the ones she has known all her life. Snowdrops and
crocuses usher in her spring. Then 'daffies' (which are
not called 'Twink', 'Dinkie' or 'Wee Bee'), tulips and
other favourites, until her big moment comes with the
moss and damask roses and the Madonna lilies. (But
during the War, and for fear they might 'draw the

bombs', she sacrificed her white lilies on the altar of Patriotism, cutting off each flower-spike before it opened.) She told me once that she liked the Regale lily; but she doesn't grow it. I am sure that in her heart of hearts she considers it (as do I) a bit *parvenu*.

They gave me, as I feared they would, a tea that they couldn't possibly afford, and strawberries with cream from a niece in Devonshire. But I think my visit gave pleasure. As for me, I always come away refreshed from that little oasis of civility and beauty and goodness. How long can it possibly last? I'm sorry if I write in a James Barrie way about them—but I just can't help it.

And now I've got what I hope and believe will be agreeable news: I'm coming up to Edinburgh for forty-eight hours! I do so want a sight of you, and to see for myself that you're really getting on as well as you say you are. I'll arrive on Wednesday night and come round to you on Thursday. I know your aunt would suggest putting me up; but she's got quite enough on her hands as it is, so I'm going to the Caledonian. I want to visit the Botanic Garden in the morning, and if you could give me lunch it would be nice. If it's a bother, then I'll come in the afternoon. I'll telephone on Wednesday evening.

Au revoir till Thursday.

P.S. The local schoolchildren have been taken to Bognor Regis for the day, and odious little Christine Peters has won the 'Say it with seaweed' competition (with half-crown prize donated by Mrs. Moon).

June 16th

It was *lovely* seeing you, and finding you in such good heart and so really better. You shouldn't have bothered to write, though of course I always hugely enjoy getting your letters. It looks as good as certain that you'll be home in the autumn, and able at last to pay that postponed visit that I so much look forward to. Hurray!

And it was nice of you to get Angus McGrath to lunch; I liked him. What with Delia and McGrath, my lifelong prejudice against everything Scottish is beginning to weaken.

You mention in your letter that you've never read Gerard's *Herball*. It's a delightful book to dip into, though I doubt if anyone has read it from cover to cover at all lately; in these days of Marathons it would make a fine endurance test. (I'll send you a small volume of 'Gleanings from'.) Gerard first appeared in

1597, and Parkinson's *Paradisus*—another lovely book
—about thirty years later. Let me give you, to be going
on with, a sample of Gerard—I'll take the bit about the
Madonna lily, so that you can compare it with E. S.
Rohde:

> The White Lilly (which in beauty and brauerie ex-
> celled *Salomon* in his greatest roialtie) hath long,
> smooth, and full bodied leaues, of a grassie or light
> greene colour. The stalks be two cubits high . . . and
> vpon them do grow faire white flowers, strong of
> smell, narrow toward the foote of the stalke whereon
> they do grow, wide or open in the mouth like a bell.
> In the middle part of them do grow small tender
> pointels tipped with a dustie yellow colour, ribbed or
> chamfered on the backe side. . . . *The Vertues.* . . . The
> root rosted in the embers and stamped with some
> leuen of rie bread & hogs grease, breaketh pestilen-
> tial botches. It ripeneth apostemes in the flankes
> comming of venerie and such like. . . .

The trouble with these early flower-books is that,
though they have enormous period charm, a little of
them goes a very long way. They're a standing temptation to what Dr. Agnes Arber used to call 'herby
women'; one can write in next to no time (and several
women have) a quite bulky, but not very readable
volume by quoting large hunks of them. The 'Vertues'
are particularly whimsical, and therefore particularly
dangerous. I imagine that about ninety-nine per cent of
the recommended treatments are valueless and many of

them positively harmful, so it's enough, in any one book, to give a couple of quotations at the most.

Did I say a couple? Well, that allows me one more piece, so here are a few lines from *A Nievve Herball*, in Henrie Lyte's translation (1578) of the original 'Doutche or Almaigne' of Dodoens. He is speaking of the 'Indian Gillofer' (African marigold), whose leaves and flowers have 'a naughtie strong & unpleasant savour', and I'll write it in my best Black Letter so as to give you the full flavour of it:

> The Indian Gillofer is very dangerous, hurtfull, and venemous, both to man and beast, as I haue tried by experience, namely upon a yong Catt, whereunto I haue giuen of these floures to eate, very finely pound with greene or fresh Cheese: whereupon she blasted immediately, and shortly after died.

I'm absolutely fascinated by a book I'm now reading —*Plant Autographs and their Revelations*, by a Bengali called Sir Jagadis Bose, published about forty years ago. I found it by chance in Traylen's bookshop when I was in Guildford, and I'll lend it you later.

Bose has a lovely black, reliable face (see the frontispiece) and he's a plant physiologist chiefly. You remember I wrote to you some time ago about animals, vegetables and minerals? Well—Bose has proved that the gaps between these three kingdoms are much narrower than was generally supposed. He found that metals get tired (what is now called 'metal fatigue', I suppose), can be stimulated by drugs and 'killed' by poisons. He discovered that in some ways plants are more sensitive than animals, and horrified the vegetarian Bernard Shaw by showing him, on his 'Death Recorder', the convulsions of a cabbage as it was being scalded to death.

Of course he experimented with the Sensitive Plant, and also with the Telegraph Plant (*Desmodium gyrans*) which I am now growing from Thompson and Morgan's seed. Apparently the Telegraph Plant, when the temperature gets above 70° F., *signals with its leaves* as if it were semaphoring from the vegetable world to the animal! And even Bose couldn't find out why.

Bose, who loved constructing ingenious instruments, made a Resonant Recorder which proved that the Sensitive Plant was far more sensitive to electric shock, and to both infra-red and ultra-violet waves, than man. So he concluded that 'the pretensions of man and animal to greater sensitiveness than their despised "vegetable brethren" does not bear the test of close scrutiny.' I was also interested to learn that all plants are 'practically deaf', so that deafness cannot be the reason why almond trees do better in towns than most other trees!

With one of his ingenious instruments Bose showed that small doses of alcohol stimulated plants, while larger doses produced 'a ludicrously unsteady gait'. But temperance reformers will be sorry to learn that the effects of too much water were even worse and led to total paralysis. He found the carrot 'highly-strung, excitable and vigorous in its responses', but celery tired so rapidly that he had to give up using it.

o

That's as far as I've got at present. I'll let you know more later.

Are you as incompetent as I am at identifying a wild flower in the botany books? The words 'botanical description', says Reginald Farrer, 'arouse shivers in the boldest', and I heartily agree. Yesterday I found a little orchid I didn't know, and tried to look it up in Clapham, Tutin and Warburg's *Flora of the British Isles*—a work which, a few years back, I was foolishly talked into buying by a very keen botanist (I say 'foolishly', because it's quite beyond me). I turned to the Orchidaceae and found myself confronted at once by a spate of those unanswerable questions: 'Are the cauticles of the pollinia attached to the rostellar viscidium?' 'Is the labellum differentiated into hypochile and epichile?' 'Is the pollen in tetrads?' and so on. I put the book back on the shelf and took down Bentham and Hooker; but I remained baffled. Were the tubers entire? I couldn't say, having always been told not to dig up rare plants. So in despair I turned to the gaudily coloured plates of what the French call an *ouvrage de vulgarisation*, and immediately recognized my flower as the narrow or sword-leaved helleborine (*Cephalanthera longifolia*) something of a rarity, I gather.

I really *do* understand and appreciate that scientists must often, to save time and space, use technical terms —maddening though they are to the layman, and especially to a non-classic like myself. But *why* need they write 'suberous, chartaceous or coriaceous' when all they mean is 'corky, papery or leathery'? Why call a fruit 'luteolus and pyriform' rather than 'yellowish and pear-shaped? Do scientists suffer from inferiority complexes, and therefore deliberately resort to this kind of hocus-pocus to impress and mystify? I feel too angry to write more on the subject; in any case, Ruskin has said it all already, and far better than ever I could.

But returning to our orchids, here is a pleasant piece from a botanical work by Jakob Breyne, published in Danzig in 1678. Oakes Ames, the great American orchidologist, translates it:

> If nature ever showed her playfulness in the formation of plants, this is visible in the most striking way among the orchids. . . . [Their flowers] take the form of little birds, of lizards, of insects. They look like a man, like a woman, sometimes like an austere, sinister fighter, sometimes like a clown who excites our laughter. They represent the image of a lazy tortoise, a melancholy toad, an agile, ever chattering monkey. Nature has formed orchid flowers in such a way that, unless they make us laugh, they surely excite our greatest admiration. The causes of their marvelous variety are (at least in my opinion) hidden by nature under a sacred veil.

'Orchis,' as you probably know, is the Greek for 'testicle', and it was Theophrastus who, about 300 B.C., chose the name, which refers of course to the twin tubers of many European orchids. Some of the popular names of British orchids are very 'curious' (as booksellers say); and you'll remember that of the 'long purples' that grew beside Ophelia's stream, Shakespeare wrote that 'liberal shepherds' gave them 'a grosser name'.

Here are a few orchidaceous lines, from an article by Oakes Ames, upon which you might care to ponder at your leisure:

> When a plant of 'Monachanthus viridis' (in reality the female of *Catasetum tridentatum*) produced male flowers clearly referable to *Catasetum tridentatum*; and when a plant of *Catasetum barbatum* (*Myanthus barbatus*) produced simultaneously in a single raceme typical male flowers and females supposedly referable to *Monachanthus viridis* but in reality females of *Catasetum barbatum*, it was thought that two male forms (representing the genera Catasetum and Myanthus) were associated with a single female form, namely a species of Monachanthus. Thus it was assumed that *Catasetum tridentatum*, *Monachanthus viridis* and *Myanthus barbatus* were all referable to *Catasetum barbatum* (*Myanthus barbatus*).

P.S. Susanna has been plaguing me to write a poem for her to translate into Armenian, so I've sent her the following:

> Fair Daffodils, we wept to see
> You haste away so soon,
> For all our superplastic ones
> Are still in flower in June.

I wonder what the Armenian for 'superplastic' is.

June 22nd

Less than a fortnight ago I was having tea with Phoebe Lawrence, and today I've been to her funeral. Carrie found her the other morning, lying dead among her flowers. She couldn't have suffered, and how could she have died better? One of those clergymen who don't gabble the lines and look all the time at their wristwatches, took the service. Emily and Carrie were very brave—just an understandable tear as they dropped their lilies on the coffin. The niece, who came up from Devonshire, was efficient about arrangements but hard and quite without charm; she must get the hard side from her mother, I suppose.

'I was this morning surprised to observe, amongst Sir Brooke Boothby's valuable collection of plants at Ashbourn, the manifest adultery of several females of the plant Collinsonia, who had bent themselves into contact with the males of other flowers of the same plant in the vicinity, neglectful of their own'—this is from a footnote in that glorious but absurd poem, *The Botanic Garden*, written around 1790 by Erasmus Darwin, grandfather of the greater Charles. Do you know it?

In the second part of the poem, 'The Loves of the Plants', Darwin describes the sex life of flowers, with stamens and pistils masquerading as beaux and belles. For example, of the broom, which has ten stamens and one pistil, he writes,

> Sweet blooms GENISTA in the myrtle shade,
> And *ten* fond brothers woo the haughty maid.

It's almost entirely in mock-heroic couplets of this kind, and the best-known, and most ridiculous, line is probably

> Gigantic Nymph! the fair KLEINHOVIA reigns . . .

the Kleinhovia being a very large Indian tree that neither you nor I have ever seen.

I've had an enormous letter from Susanna from Naples, full of incoherence and ecstasy. She has got so far without losing anything except (my copy of) Baedeker's *Southern Italy*—which must be a record; Delia has always maintained that her incompetence was largely a pose, but I never believed her.

In Venice Susanna wrote a *Hymn to the Virgin Mary* (which unfortunately has *not* been lost), and was so overwhelmed by the quantity of churches that on leaving she asked her gondolier to conduct her to the 'Santa Stazione'. In Florence 'all the men looked like Michelangelo's "David",' though presumably on a smaller scale and more fully clothed. In Rome she saw the Pope on his balcony (from a quarter of a mile away) and observed 'an air of sympathy in the eye' (she doesn't say which). In Naples, on what must have been an exceptionally dark night, she was picked up by an Italian sailor on the water-front. At Pompei a tout attempted to sell her some photographs which, though she wrote 'as artist to artist', she preferred to leave undescribed. She is due back tomorrow, when she will no doubt describe them.

Bose may have proved, scientifically, how small a gap there is between animal, vegetable and mineral; but St. Francis of Assissi, with his 'Brother Wind' and 'Sister Water', had reached the same conclusion, by quite other argument, a good seven hundred years earlier. And so had the Chinese and the Japanese, with their courtesy to Nature and their instinctive feeling that man wasn't superior to flowers and insects. Don't you agree that in general the West still spells Nature with a small 'n'? Here's Chekov neatly summing up the Western attitude:

> Lubkov was fond of nature, but he looked upon it as something long familiar and at the same time infinitely inferior to himself and created for his pleasure. Sometimes he would stand in front of a magnificent view and say, 'How nice it would be to have tea here!'

Contrast this with the Japanese poem about the poor pilgrim on the highroad who stopped beating his bell lest the sound might shake a single petal from the cherries. Can you see Mrs. Puttenham holding her fire under similar circumstances? Lord Pheen, on the other hand, might. And there is the yet better-known poem about the girl who went to draw water from her well, but finding that overnight a convolvulus had twined itself around the bucket and rope, came away, her pitcher empty, to seek 'gift-water' instead.

You can find such lovely things about flowers in Arthur Waley's translations from the Chinese, and elsewhere in Far Eastern literature. Islam hasn't so much to offer. There's a traditional saying of Mahomet's: 'If you have two loaves of bread, sell one and buy a narcissus for the good of your soul.' But do you think it carries conviction? Frankly I don't.

I've only just remembered that you asked me some time ago about the Biblical lily. Both the Old Testament lily (Hebrew *shushan*) and the New Testament lily (Greek *krinon*) undoubtedly covered a lot of different plants, and the only occasion when there is the least likelihood of the Madonna lily being meant is in the mention of 'lily work' on the capitals of the pillars in the Temple porch (I Kings, vii, 19). When Solomon said he was 'the lily of the valleys' he certainly wasn't referring to the humble *Convallaria majalis*, which in any case isn't a Palestinian plant. As for the New Testament lilies—I haven't the slightest doubt in my own mind that when Jesus said, 'Consider the lilies of the field', He simply meant, 'Look at the wild flowers,' and that it's sheer folly to pretend, as many Biblical commentators do, that He was inviting His audience specifically to observe *Sternbergia lutea* or *Anemone fulgens* or any particular iris or tulip. Did you know that the botanists now maintain that Eve tempted Adam with an apricot?

The only local news is that Daphne Usher is engaged to that dumb Australian I met at the Stringers'. Usher is believed to approve of the match; but Daphne will have to live in Australia, and it's thought that he'll be absolutely lost without her.

It's suddenly become wintry here, and tonight I have a fire. How I agree with Horace Walpole that in our climate, winter or summer, 'the best sun we have is made of Newcastle coal, and I am determined never to reckon upon any other'. Incidentally, if, as the calendars say, summer begins on June 21st and Midsummer's Day is June 24th, then surely summer should end on June 27th. I hope we shall get our week's ration at some time or other this year, and preferably before the old roses are over.

June 29th

> What's this I hear,
> My Flora dear,
>   About the new Carnivora?
> Can little plants
> Eat bugs and ants,
> And gnats and flies?
> Who is the wise,
>   Who is the great 'diskiverer'?

Actually, my very dear Flora, the poem is addressed to 'Molly', but 'Flora' fits just as well; I copied it out years ago and don't know where it comes from. I remembered it when I was reading the other day about some experiments made by Mrs Hughes-Gibb on sundews—'small ruddy plants', she calls them. (I think I mentioned her name once before, in connection with bean-leaves.) I'm sure you know the common sundew, with the red, gum-tipped tentacles that close round the insects that settle on them.

While on holiday with her family at Chagford, Mrs. Hughes-Gibb decided to find out what the sundew could and could not assimilate. She potted one and fed it for three days—first with red wine, then with whisky, and on the third day with methylated spirits. By this time it was looking 'very unhealthy', so she gave it, of all things, Devonshire cream—which the plant ultimately 'ejected'!

For some reason or other she decided that sundews liked whisky, which she poured on them from her pocket flask where they grew on the moors; but the results of her experiment were 'rather inconclusive'. Others she chloroformed—with little effect. She found that sundews accepted cooked veal, mutton, chicken and fish, and raw meat in small quantities. (Another investigator observed that they were 'very partial to rump-steak'.) White of egg they were able to digest, but it left a black deposit on the leaves. Mrs. Hughes-Gibb's principal conclusion was that sundews can't assimilate fat.

You say I've never mentioned Mrs. Leighton. Poor Pamela counts for so little that she's easily overlooked. I believe the money is mostly hers, but it was Eric who bought the house—without her even having seen it. Pamela likes town life and theatres and concerts, but Eric never even takes her to the Guildford Rep. Eric never goes away because he won't leave his garden, and Pamela can't ever go away because Eric won't be left alone. She's older than he—sixty, perhaps—and pretty tired of her husband and of life in general I suspect.

The other day I found myself passing near Ashton's Bottom and called in. Eric was out, but Pamela took me into the garden. I noticed, near the house, a cistus that I didn't know, flowering so freely that I wondered why Eric hadn't had it out. Without thinking, I picked a flower to examine it. Pamela was horrified—and rather frightened. 'I wish you hadn't done that,' she said. 'Eric doesn't like anything being picked without his permission.' Of course I apologized. But I couldn't resist saying, 'Do you mean that you can't pick a bunch of flowers for the house without asking him first? 'Oh no! He wouldn't like that at all!' Poor woman! I remembered that Helen Parker had told me that Eric made his wife drag the lawn-mower bare-footed (while he steered), so that she should feel the stones and save damage to the blades. Helen has a lively imagination, but it could almost be true.

Susanna is back, having lost nothing *en route* except my Baedeker; I shall waste no more sympathy on her incompetence in this respect. She was round here at once, of course—clutching a fistful of post-cards and a hideous Carrara-marble ash-tray-cum-dove that she'd bought for me in Pisa. She stayed for four hours. It was clear that her 'accostation' (as she called it) in Naples was the high-light of her trip, but I was thankful that she made no attempt to discuss the Pompeian photographs: Susanna is *not* the kind of person with whom one would choose to share an improper joke.

Here is a little thumb-nail sketch of village life for you. Delia said it would be a great kindness if I called in on old Mrs. Anderson, who is tied by the leg in a small cottage, and introduced myself. 'You could take her a few flowers; but I warn you she's *desperately* shy.' So I picked a bunch of roses and went and knocked on her door.

Mrs. Anderson presumably said, 'Come in!' but it sounded more like 'Get out!'

'Good afternoon, Mrs. Anderson,' I said. Mrs. Lovell told me you might like a visitor. My name's Sharp and I live at Orchards, where Mr. Trotter used to live. I've brought you a few roses.'

Mrs. Anderson said, 'Yes'.

'What a pretty room you've got! I *do* admire your lustre jugs.'

Mrs. Anderson said, 'Yes'.

'Have you lived in Dewbury all your life?'

Mrs. Anderson said, 'No'.

I paused, baffled. Suddenly Mrs. Anderson blurted out, prestissimo, 'Have-you-ever-been-to-the-west-coast-of-Ireland?'

I told her that I hadn't. No doubt it was very beautiful, the white-washed cottages, fuchsias everywhere, etc., etc.

Mrs. Anderson said, 'Neither have I.'

After that I gave up.

You told me that McGrath collects stamps (he ought to have outgrown that by now; it's a kid's game—or worse, a speculators' racket)—so I thought you might like to give him these curious Cuban ones which came on a letter yesterday.

Ever your very affectionate godfather

Wilfrid Sharp

JULY

My dearest Flora,

I've been meaning to tell you about two guests I had to lunch last month—on different days, I mean. The contrast couldn't have been greater.

One was old Lady St. Hubert—a shocking old harridan with hair dyed the colour of Oxford marmalade: the nastiest kind of snob. I only invited her because George Leamington, who is a friend of mine, told me that his mother was adjacent and lonely—Lord St. Hubert having, very sensibly, gone off to South Africa without her. Such a woman deserves to be lonely. Mrs. Puttenham is a snob because she is vulgar and parvenue; Lady St. Hubert has no such excuse: she comes from one of the oldest families in England and married into another of them. She surveyed me with the distaste of a preparatory school matron who suspects a small boy of not having washed behind the ears.

'George,' she announced pompously to Delia, who was also lunching with me—'George has made a very satisfactory marriage; I wish I could say the same of my daughters. I always hoped that one of them would marry a moor——'

'What!' Delia couldn't resist saying; 'like Desdemona?'

Lady St. Hubert ignored the interruption and continued acidly, 'and the other a trout stream'. Then she turned her attack on me: 'I could give your cook a few hints on how to make a *soufflé*; *and* it's cold.'

(The first hint, I longed to say, would be to allow for Lady St. Hubert being thirty-five minutes late for lunch.)

After a couple of hours of her, during most of which Delia and I were subjected to a monologue on the superiority of everything of hers to everything of mine, I began to wish that the French Revolution had crossed the Channel and exterminated her and her breed. But not George Leamington, who is absolutely delightful; funny, as Saki says somewhere, how these things sometimes skip a generation. Or perhaps George takes after his father.

My other guest was Lord Pheen, and we went on afterwards to Sissinghurst—fifty miles, but we did it in an hour and a half. I admit that there are still a lot of famous English gardens I haven't seen, and I hardly know the Scottish and Irish ones at all; but of those that I *have* seen, I put Sissinghurst top. And Pheen entirely agreed with me. As he rightly said, so few of the great gardens have been created by *artists*—and Vita Sackville-West is an artist to her fingertips. There are plenty of gardens that are well designed and which 'obey the rules', where trees and shrubs are superbly grown and vistas nicely calculated; but so often they just lack that touch of genius which lifts them out of the 'fine garden' class into the magical. Pheen could hardly be dragged away from the silver and white garden, which was just at its most perfect. The Nicolsons made us welcome, as always, and insisted on our coming in to tea with them although we had brought a thermos in the car.

I wish I'd had a tape-recorder to preserve Lady Nicolson's conversation with Pheen as we went round the garden. It was impressionist talk: a touch here, a touch there, bringing each plant in turn to life. And I wish I could see more of Pheen. But, friendly though he always is, I think he prefers solitude and the company of his flowers.

Delia and Humphrey are now on Loch Fyne, where they have a derelict lodge, and a sailing dinghy in which they sail about the West Coast sleeping where they can, in farms and cottages or even 'à la belle étoile'. Quite extraordinary! Delia wrote me a postcard, 'Once a laurel green wave followed us for so long that I longed to give it a biscuit, but Humphrey thought it might encourage it to come on board. So I went on baling water and trying to think of a name for a race horse, a filly; Cochineal—Fish Paste. Can you? And don't say "Red Herring" because it's been used already. Our cook has a baby and can think of nothing else but vintage dill-water . . .' Her letters are a joy; somebody ought to publish a selection of them—but not so long as Mesdames Moon and Puttenham are still alive.

We've just had our annual village flower show, where most of the prizes were of course won by Mrs. Puttenham—in other words, by Chandler. But Delia, I'm glad to say, beat her in the Carnation class, Mrs. P.'s carnations having wilted in the night because somebody ('an enemy hath done this'?) had put a large plate of apples next them. Did you know that the gases given off by apples killed carnations?

A lot of distinguished horticulturists, William Robinson and Gertrude Jekyll among them, have deplored the very existence of flower shows. Robinson always refused to exhibit, and Miss Jekyll pours almost Ruskinian venom on those who put beauty aside 'in favour of set rules and measurements' and who produce flowers 'teased and tortured and fatted and bloated into ugly and useless monstrosities'. And I always like the remark made by one of Saki's characters: 'so patronizing and irritating to the Almighty, I should think, to go about putting superior finishing touches to Creation.' It's worse than ever today. There are dahlias now as big as tea-trays, delphiniums as tall as lamp-posts, and begonias as plump and pink as primadonnas, all of which resemble their prototypes about as much as an all-in wrestler resembles the Apollo Belvedere.

Of course the little man wants his delphiniums taller than those of the little man next door, just as he wants a noisier wireless and his wife a more expensive washing-machine and a whiter detergent. But surely there ought

P

to be more people who know better, and who see that it's largely a nurserymen's racket. I'm only surprised that the nurserymen haven't yet got on to the possibilities of hire-purchase.

Well, I watched the judges, all looking tremendously self-important, going the rounds, and I'm sure that you too would have thought the winning 'floral arrangement' —zinnias and fig-leaves in an old football boot—*too* much of a bad thing. I've already given you my views about flower arrangements, so now I'll let off steam about the 'rules' that competition judges have laid down —quite arbitrarily, as I see it—for the judging of flowers. Let me take the iris.

It appears to be agreed, by iris experts, that irises (they are thinking of varieties of *Iris germanica*) should avoid certain 'faults'. Mr. Leslie Cave[1] says that they should not have strongly marked stripes on the hafts of the falls (he must mean, on the upper part of the falls) because these are 'a blot on the flower's beauty, since they . . . take up space *which could be put to better use*' (my italics). He says that 'a stumpy stem bearing large flowers, or a tall stem with small flowers, will look wrong. They [*sic*] will lack proportion. So also will a flower with large standards and small falls.' He says that the falls must not 'recurve' (i.e., turn in at the bottom), because this will 'hide a certain amount of the colour'.

Now why should the 'experts' lay down the law in this way? I know you know *Iris atrofusca*, because we

[1] *The Iris*, by N. Leslie Cave; Faber, 1950.

admired it together once at an R.H.S. show. To my mind it is one of the most beautifully formed and excitingly proportioned of all flowers—yet it breaks every one of the above-mentioned 'regulations'. Why should varieties of *Iris germanica* be obliged to follow a pattern dictated by the 'experts', when God has shown that he can produce a masterpiece iris by breaking all their rules?

Mr. Cave gives photographs in his book of six 'faulty' irises, of which the sixth of this 'chamber of horrors' (as he calls it) is singled out as the most horrible: 'This is appalling . . . falls tuck under and twist, etc.' Now to my mind this particular 'tuck and twist' of the falls has a curious charm, a kind of gothic crispness—and I believe that any artist, as opposed to 'iris expert', will understand what I mean. Certainly Jacopo Bellini did—as his lovely drawing of an iris, now in the Louvre, shows. Why should we be dictated to like this?

I choose the iris because I was particularly angry at the judges' decision in this class (no—I wasn't competing!). All I have said applies equally to other flowers; and no doubt to dogs as well, though I know nothing about dog shows. But I've been looking at irises for nearly forty years. I've passed what Mr. Cave calls 'the adolescent phase'. He says there are 'no rigid rules to which irises must conform if they are to pass muster', and then proceeds to lay down such rules. I grow an iris I collected on the shores of the Caspian, which tucks its falls under and twists in a most un-Cave-like manner; but I think it beautiful and I shall continue to grow it. I will *not* be bullied! I will *not* have Mr. Cave holding a *pistil* at my head!

You may enjoy, in this connection, an almost inconceivably piece of arrogance written by a Mr. Glenny in *The Floricultural Cabinet* for 1848:

> I beg to call the attention of the readers to the simple fact that no writer on the Tulip ever hinted a word as to the form being circular or globular in any proportion whatever . . . until I in 1832, and often since that period, laid down as a principle, that the form should be from one-third to one-half of a hollow ball. . . . When those writers who found their credit upon what they purloin from others have been forgotten, my standard will remain as mine and mine only. . . . I consider all the miserable attempts to describe the same proportions in different words very contemptible, and such is the opinion of the leading enthusiasts in floriculture.

I said I'd tell you about the 'snarers'. The Portuguese sundew (*Drosophyllum lusitanicum*) doesn't behave like the true sundews: insects are caught by the stickiness; but the tentacles don't close, so it can't be classed among the hunters. However, it is the one insectivorous plant which has been definitely proved to *digest* its food in the way that an animal does. The Portuguese use their sundews as fly-papers.

Most of the snarers—the bladderworts, pitcher-plants, sarracenias, darlingtonias and nepenthes—rely on pitfalls of the lobster-pot kind. They vary enormously in detail, but the general principle is more or less uniform: a bait, honeyed or brightly-coloured, leads to a slippery cavity lined with downward-pointing bristles and filled with a decomposing fluid. The insects enter, descend (*facilis descensus Averno*), and cannot return.

Some of these insectivorous plants are marvellous, and when you're south again we must go to Kew and look at them. You probably already know the tropical nepenthes and aristolochias (Dutchman's pipes). The sarracenias—North American bog-plants—are like old-fashioned ear-trumpets; the mouths of the trumpets are exquisitely veined in green and wine-colour. There are two splendid pictures of American insectivorous plants in Thornton's *Temple of Flora*.

Cobaea is roaring up my wall, its mobiles (which are midrib-tendrils, like the sweet pea's) pawing the air till they find a hold. It's now grown about seven feet, and the flanged buds are showing. The moonflowers in the greenhouse are equally flourishing. I've found a bit in Charles Kingsley's *At Last* about the moonflower in the West Indies. Comparing it with the Carolinea (whatever that is) he writes, 'Even more swiftly fades an even more delicate child of the moon, the Ipomoea Bona-nox, whose snow-white patines, as broad as the hand, open at nightfall on every hedge, and shrivel up with the first rays of dawn.

And now Patrick Synge has sent me a piece from *The Gardens of Taprobane*, by the Count de Mauny. The Count, describing his garden in Ceylon, writes of the 'beautiful cream-coloured clove-scented cups, as large as plates, which unfurl at sunset and last until the following morning. The effect by moonlight is indescribable. How often have I watched the buds unfurl their spirals, counting twenty while the flower opened! They run in garlands along the heavy ropes which join the columns around the roof-garden'. He says that they flower from seed in a month, and that by monthly sowings he can have them in flower all the year round except at the height of the north-west monsoon.

'From moonflowers to Moons'—this is the kind of fatuous remark that the Light Programme is so fond of. Last night I had a nightmare: I found myself marrying (the presumedly widowed) Mrs. Moon! As we stood side by side in the centre aisle, Mrs. Moon nudged me and whispered, 'Do you realize you're wearing your old gardening trousers?' I saw to my horror that I was. And then I noticed that the side aisles of the church were filled with the largest flowering trees and shrubs from my garden—the fifteen-foot lilacs, the big Judas tree, the davidia, and so on. I think you once told me that you never have nightmares. I envy you!

What an interminable letter!

And even now, a P.S.! Did you happen to see that the R.H.S. has recently given an award to Cox's Orange Pippin? I wonder if it feels flattered at receiving, at the age of about a hundred, this belated pat-on-the-back; it's as though the National Book League were suddenly to announce, with a great flourish of trumpets, its discovery that *Vanity Fair* was rather a good novel.

July 12th

Sorry! I didn't mean to sound so offensive about the suburban gardener, whose enthusiasm and knowledge I greatly admire. I only meant that he could have so much more fun, and so much more cheaply, if he wasn't always trying to outstrip the Gardiner-Joneses. Country cottage gardens, full of plants that have very likely been growing there for generations, are often so lovely. There are more keen small-gardeners in England than in all the rest of the world put together, and I hope that those architects who plan to house us compulsorily in top-heavy thirty-storey white boxes with a communal garden, will be properly discouraged.

Now climbing plants. Wouldn't you love to see a tropical forest with lianas writhing and twining like snakes? After watching my cobaea roaring upwards, I started to read about the different techniques that climbing plants use to advance themselves in the world.

There are the weavers—blackberries, for example— which infiltrate through the undergrowth and establish themselves at every stage by putting out side-branches and by making use of barbs and thorns. Some of the climbing roses (for instance *Rosa setigera*, the prairie rose) have a curious property which helps them to get up trellised walls: the young shoots avoid the light and so hide behind the trellis; but when they mature they *need* light and come out again through the trellis at a higher point.

Then there are the lattice-makers, mostly tropical, which construct their own trellises as they go along. There are the twiners: the tropical twiners that either strangle a young tree to death or are themselves burst asunder by the tree's expanding stem; our gentler climbers—the bindweeds, hop, honeysuckle and so on. How curious, incidentally, that the hop and the honeysuckle should spiral clockwise, the scarlet-runner and the bindweeds anti-clockwise, and that neither heat nor light nor dampness nor the hand of man can make them alter their habits! I expect you've seen one of those quick-motion films (which most people call *slow*-motion) showing the tip of a twining plant swinging round, like the lash of a whip, until it finds a support and begins to climb. The tip of a hop can make a complete revolution in about two hours in warm weather, and you can actually see it move.

True climbers, like the ivies, make new roots as they climb. Cobaea, like the bryony, climbs by means of tendrils—and what wonderful tendrils they are! They look like mobiles made of the finest flexible wire, each final branch ending in a double claw whose points fasten into any object, even the skin of the hand, at the slightest touch. The tendrils of the Virginian creeper have adhesive discs which can stick to a smooth wall; but some of the self-clinging climbers need a rough wall with crevices in which the tips of the tendrils can embed themselves.

The only local news is that Eric has been lecturing to our Gardening Society on 'Erica, or Little by Little'—in other words, his lifelong flirtation with the heath family, whose species he has been gradually revising and renaming. There were eighteen of us present. I sat next to Mrs. Montgomery, who admitted to me afterwards that she hadn't known what an erica was—and I don't think she was the only one; possibly she imagined it was a plant that had been named after Eric.

Eric had taken enormous trouble over his talk, which he read from a long typescript in a very dead voice. There were no slides and, except for the title of his talk, no trace of humour. If he hadn't brought two or three plants with him, I think Mrs. Montgomery might have gone home without ever discovering that erica just meant heather. Helen Parker tells me that the lecture is to be given to the R.H.S. and that this was a 'try-out'.

I don't think that Eric had the least idea that the evening hadn't been a success—not even after the awful silence that followed when he invited questions. (But poor Pamela realized it.) At last, in desperation, Helen —who is the Secretary—asked what the word 'ling' came from. It was an unhappy shot: Eric didn't know.

A friend of mine who's just flown back from Jamaica had brought me a small bunch of a most exotic-looking flower. We neither of us knew what it was, and as I was going to Eric's lecture I stuck one in my jacket. Eric eyed it curiously and said, 'What's that *inflorescence* in your button-hole?'

Of course we all know that there's a difference between 'flower' and 'inflorescence', but—well, it was so absolutely *typical* of Eric! Had Eric written *Patience*, his pedantry would have made him put:

> If you walk down Piccadilly, London, W.1,
> With an inflorescence of *Papaver orientale* L. or
> *Lilium candidum* L.

and that would have made things a bit difficult for Sullivan!

I have the feeling that Ovenden and I will have to part company. Mrs. Benham announced yesterday that he was 'a funny one'—the very words, curiously enough, that Ovenden used last week to describe Mrs. Benham. But Ovenden is certainly *not* my idea of fun. It isn't that he's such a bad gardener—though he doesn't know half as much as he imagines he does; but he's idle, pigheaded, and *never* in the wrong. Also he's a liar. I can forgive him for swearing that he actually heard a mandrake shriek when he pulled it up; but some of his lies are tiresome as well as silly. When I pointed to a bed that needed weeding, he declared that he'd completely cleared it of weeds a week ago. 'Don't blame me, Sir! It's the bomb.' Yesterday he marched triumphantly up to me, clutching a fasciated piece of forsythia. 'What did I tell you, Sir! Just look at that! You can't do nothing with all them geranium bombs about.'

P.S. How *dare* you call me a snob, just because I happened to mention two titled people in the same letter!

July 16th

Rather unwisely, I mentioned to Ovenden that the
mandrake was not an English plant, and that I'd never
seen it growing in this country or even listed in a
nurseryman's catalogue. I added that, according to the
legend, anyone who pulled one up, or who merely
heard one shriek, dropped dead. I explained the ritual of
its gathering: how the collector stuffed his ears with
wax, tied a famished dog to the plant, enticed the
animal forward with a slab of raw meat and so got it to
pull the root out of the ground—the dog, of course,
dropping dead. But Ovenden would not budge: 'I tell
you, Sir, I *'eard* 'im cry—cry just like a baby!'

You probably know something at any rate about
mandrakes, whose forked roots have the appearance of
a man, or of a woman (woman-drake). The legends
about the plant are legion, and date back at least to the
Book of Genesis (see chapter xxx), when Rachel availed
herself of its reputed aphrodisiac properties. (What is
more, Biblical commentators seem agreed that the mandrake of Genesis really *was* our modern mandrake *Man-
dragora officinarum.*) The Rachel story is complicated
and not very edifying. Reuben, the son of Rachel's
sister Leah, brought in some mandrakes from the
fields. Rachel, who was barren, agreed that Leah might
'hire', for a single night, their joint husband Jacob (who
much preferred Rachel) in exchange for a few mandrakes. The plant lived up to its reputation: Leah gave
birth to Issachar, and in due course Rachel bore Joseph.

With no mandrake, and therefore no Joseph, Old Testament history would have been a very different story.

You must read C. J. S. Thompson's *The Mystic Mandrake*. It gives the history of the mandrake cult in all parts of Europe and Asia, even as far as China. It tells you how to manipulate the roots to make them look more human, and how to palm off bryony roots if you can't get hold of the genuine article. It explains how to keep your mandrake in good shape—e.g. by bathing it regularly on Fridays. It gives a list of its magical properties, and apparently there's hardly an ailment or a predicament where the mandrake doesn't come in useful (for instance, you can't lose a law-suit if you are carrying one in the right armpit). I must try to get hold of one for you!

What, by the way, are your views on flag days? Mrs. Stringer came round this morning, when I had hardly digested my breakfast, selling flags in aid of the Dumb Friends League. Personally I don't much care for this particular form of extortion, which is steadily on the increase in England; in France I believe they have the thing properly under control. It's not that I disapprove of these societies that succour animals in distress (though I do think that they often behave unwisely); in fact I'm an annual subscriber to the R.S.P.C.A. But I can't see why one should be *shamed* into giving—for that's what it amounts to, and I can't really believe that money thus contributed can lay up much treasure in heaven for the contributor. Nor do I think that Mrs.

Stringer showed salesmanship in bringing with her her green mongrel, whose bite can hardly be worse than its bark. Renoir, when dogs came yapping round him, used to say that he approved of the Chinese custom of eating them: there are moments when I am inclined to agree with him. In fact, the trouble with our dumb friends is that so few of them *are* dumb.

Then Mrs. Stringer insisted upon my going round to see her salvias. She's clever at making things grow—much cleverer than I am, but she's no taste and I couldn't help wondering whether she mightn't be colourblind. Admittedly she *talked* a lot about colour, how you couldn't go wrong if you 'followed the order of the spectrum—Nature's way' (which sounded like an advertisement for a laxative), and how dangerous it was to grow scarlet and magenta flowers near together; but these are just things that she's picked up parrot-wise: she doesn't *feel* them. I suggested that Nature must have been napping when she designed some of the fuchsias, and said I often found clashing colours exciting—like the discords of Stravinsky; but she replied that she was afraid she wasn't 'educated up to modern art'. So I gave up: 'Mit der Dummheit,' said Schiller, 'kämpfen Götter selbst vergebens.' She herself underplants Paul's Scarlet roses with marigolds 'because orange comes next to red in the spectrum', and they were flowering ferociously together: the spectrum obviously has some kind of a mystique for her. 'You must agree that my garden is *colourful*,' she said. It is—just as a pigsty is 'smelful'.

July 19th

How hard it is, isn't it, to find agreement in gardening books about the right way to plant even the simplest bulb!

I've been putting in three dozen colchicum corms in the wilderness, and before doing so I consulted various books and catalogues. Blom recommends planting 'not less than four inches deep and three inches apart', while E. A. Bowles says they do best 'with the cap of the tunic reaching the surface'. Last time I put them six inches down (which I read somewhere) and they did perfectly, so I've done the same again.

Naturally people don't agree about the leaves: the catalogues call them 'bold-looking and very effective', whereas Bowles found them 'almost annoying' when they unfolded in spring. That's just a question of taste or salesmanship. Personally I like them—in the wild.

I've loved colchicums ever since I first saw them—which was in the meadows of Alsace in 1920; and I can't count the number of times I've enjoyed them since, especially in southern Germany and northern Italy. The Germans call them 'Nackte Mädchen'; not knowing this, I was surprised when my Bavarian hostess told me she had put 'a few naked maidens' in my bedroom. In French they are 'tue-chiens' (dog-killers—I ought to have planted a few where the Stringers' mongrel comes through!), 'culs tout nus' (bare bottoms) and such like. In England—where I've never seen them wild, though in places they're quite common—they're most usually 'autumn crocus' or 'naked boys', but also, locally, 'upstarts', 'daggers', 'kite's legs', 'naked nannies' and so on. Old Parkinson (quoting from Gerard's *Herball*) wrote, 'Some haue called them also *Filius ante Patrem*, the Sonne before the Father, because (as they thinke) it giueth seede before the flower', but comments that this is 'without due consideration'. It certainly is, because the seeds follow with the leaves in the spring. The Arabs call them 'lamps of the ghoul', and the ancient Assyrians—no, I can't tell you that!

Certainly there was never a nakeder flower—but if planted in grass this doesn't matter. What I love are not the fat colchicums that look like purple electric-light bulbs, but the exquisitely graceful *Colchicum autumnale*, and the little tessellated *C. agrippinum* which for some extraordinary reason it appears to be almost impossible to buy.

As you probably know, the colchicum is extremely

poisonous, especially the corm ('isschewe it', wrote Turner). Dioscorides (in Goodyear's seventeenth-century translation) says that it 'killeth by choking like to ye mushrumps'—by which I suppose he means poisonous fungi. But it's also the source of a valuable drug, colchicine, and Sir Theodore Mayerne successfully treated King James I's gout with it—mixed with the powder of unburied skulls. It's odd that the old herbalists, who believed in the Doctrine of Signatures, didn't notice how like the colchicum was to a gouty foot.

And doubtless you also know that the colchicum is a Lily, whereas the crocus is an Iris and the sternbergia a Daffodil—though in general appearance all three are very much alike. I use capitals because I mean that the colchicum is a member of the Lily family (Liliaceae), not of course a true lily (Lilium). It's so convenient being able to talk about an orchid—meaning one of the Orchidaceae, and so inconvenient not having a corresponding word for a Lily, or indeed for members of most other families. The result is that botanists sometimes take the matter into their own hands and refer familiarly to, say, a 'scroph' (one of the Scrophulariaceae)—and one can hardly blame them.

Incidentally, what a mixed bag some of these families are! Take the Lilies, for example, which include such improbables as the asparagus, the aspidistra and the ruscus (butcher's broom)—though the R.H.S. Dictionary is really going a little *too* far in including the sweet pea (Lathyrus)!

This afternoon I took our local lily, Susanna, over to

Q

Compton to see the Watts Gallery; she'd read some-where that there might be a Watts revival on the way, and she wanted to get in on the ground floor. I enjoyed watching her trying to decide whether Watts was a rising, or merely a burnt-out, star—in other words, whether or not to hitch her wagon to him. In the end she 'hitched', talked enthusiastically about his neglected 'genial', and bought a lot of postcards of 'Hope' to send to her Armenian barbed-wirists in Paris.

The Curator came into the Gallery while we were there, and I had a word with him because I'd noticed that his name was Wilfrid *Blunt*. Stranger still, we found that we were born on the same day (today, in fact) of the same month of the same year! As Susanna observed, it was almost as curious as the Charles-Char-lot relationship in the film we'd seen together at Studio Eleven. Blunt, who'd been a master at Eton for many years, said he found life very pleasant at Compton. I'm not surprised; it's a delightful spot, tucked away in greenery below the Hog's Back. (Or 'Swine's Spine', as he called it; he seemed a nice chap, but his sense of humour was a bit ponderous.) Susanna asked him how he'd come to get the job, and was he perhaps an 'ances-tor' of Watts! Really her English gets steadily worse.

Three rather ragged-looking youths came into the Gallery while we were there, and I heard one of them say to Blunt, 'Did *you* paint all these?' Blunt explained that they were painted by Watts, and that he was dead. To this the youth responded with an unanswerable question, 'Well, then 'oo paints 'em now?'

Blunt insisted upon our coming in to have a cup of tea with him (delicious cucumber sandwiches; he says he has a treasure of a housekeeper). He told me that he was sick to death of the flood-lighting and vapid historical trumpetings of 'Son et Lumière', so he proposes to hold an 'Ombre et Silence' Festival at the Watts Gallery: darkness, silence, hock, and lobster mayonnaise, with tickets at twenty guineas each and all proceeds to go to the Curator. A good idea. It certainly sounds preferable to the 'Chopin and Champagne Gala Soirée' at Chipstone, with seven guinea tickets (in aid of Greek Child Welfare) and a Greek protégé of the Duchess's at the piano. Delia went and said there was too much Chopin (she thought perhaps his complete works) and too little champagne, and that for seven guineas she felt entitled to expect something better than spam and lettuce.

The petunias I planted in that large pot near the front door having done rather poorly, I have cheered them up by adding half-a-dozen artificial hyacinths from Selfridge's. I remember a schoolmaster once telling me that he kept a reproduction of Vermeer's 'View of Delft' hanging upside-down in his hall to test the intelligence and powers of observation of his parents; I find my hyacinths equally instructive. Your mother spotted the fraud immediately and said, rather acidly, 'I don't see the *point* of them.' (If it comes to that, what's the *point* of real ones?) Nor, I observed, was Mrs. Moon deceived, but she merely averted her eyes in silent disgust from the improper spectacle. Dorothy Drake expressed surprise that hyacinths should be out in mid-summer, and added, 'but then of course you're always so *clever* with flowers'.

I can't myself see that there's anything more *improper* about artificial flowers than there is about gramophone records, coloured reproductions of paintings, travel films, TV or tinned pineapples; they're all convenient and more or less adequate substitutes for the real thing when for some reason or other it's not available. Why shouldn't the R.H.S. accept the fact that artificial flowers have come to stay, and encourage, by means of competitions, the manufacture of really good ones? The wax orchids in Museum I at Kew, made a hundred years ago, are miraculous and the collection of glass flowers at Harvard has to be seen to be believed; couldn't a method be devised for producing work of comparable quality commercially?

Yet there is evidence that I still have a shred of decency left. I don't, like Reginald Farrer, admire the blush of white irises that have been left standing in red ink. Nor shall I be ordering this winter an electrically-lit Xmas tree 'made of plastic in two-tone shades of pine green' and described as 'the rage of the U.S.A'. They must rage without me.

It was good of you to remember my birthday—a serious one, for I am entering my sixtieth year; your very welcome letter came just after I'd posted my last to you. But how on earth did *Delia* know? Only *you*, I think, can have told her. Mrs. Benham brings me my post with my early morning tea, and out of a small package addressed in Delia's smallest writing emerged a little leather stud-box. I opened the box—upside down, as it happened—and a shower of seeds fell all over me. On a scrap of paper Delia had written microscopically, 'Darling, *many* happy returns of the day! White fox-glove seed, to be scattered in your wood and *not* sown in a bed.' I shan't dare to tell her how exactly I've dis-obeyed her instructions.

Her letter continued, 'I would like to give you so many things, a tame dolphin, and a white Arab stallion with a silver bridle, and Jeunes Filles au Piano by Renoir or whatever you wanted more, and a gold snuff-box and a Ming bowl and a waistcoat made by the Tailor of Gloucester. One day I will. D.'

And now I have to wish *you* many happy returns of *your* birthday. I've sent you a book which you may like to have—Hellyer's *The Amateur Gardener*, an admirable work; if by any chance you've already got it, Hatchards will change it.

Here's some more Bose for you—part of an article in the *Nation* describing a visit its correspondent made to Bose's laboratory in London shortly before the First World War:

In a room near Maida Vale there is an unfortunate carrot strapped to the table of an unlicenced vivi-sector. Wires pass through two glass tubes full of a white substance; they are like two legs, whose feet are buried in the flesh of the carrot. When the vegetable is pinched with a pair of forceps, it winces.

It is so strapped that its electric shudder of pain pulls the long arm of a very delicate lever which actuates a tiny mirror. This casts a beam of light on the frieze at the other end of the room, and thus enormously exaggerates the tremor of the carrot. A pinch near the right-hand tube sends the beam seven or eight feet to the right, and a stab near the other will send it as far to the left. . . .

And here is an experiment that Bose made with garden peas:

Take one half of a green pea, and connect its inner and outer surfaces with a galvanometer. The half pea is slowly raised in temperature in a heating bath. At the death-point of 60° C., an intense electric discharge passes through the organism. The electric change at death is very considerable, being often as high as 0·5 volt. If 500 pairs of half-peas are suitably arranged in series, the terminal electric pressure will be 500 volts, more than sufficient to cause electrocution of unsuspecting human victims. It is well that the cook does not know the danger she runs in preparing this particular dish, and it is fortunate for her that the peas are not arranged in series!

Another instalment in due course—if you can bear it!

I've suddenly had an idea as to how you might pass some of your time, now that you're so much better: why not make a translation of Walafrid Strabo's *Hortulus* (Little Garden)? Let me start at the beginning and tell you all about it, and him.

Walafrid Strabo (Strabo means 'the squinter') lived in the ninth century and was Abbot of the Monastery on the island of Reichenau, in Lake Constance. He compiled the usual historical and theological works—now probably unreadable; but he also wrote in quite decent Latin hexameters, what is really the first book on gardening. Of course he often had Virgil's fourth Georgic in mind; but what he wrote was a practical handbook based on his own experience, and it's perfectly delightful.

Having taken on a derelict bit of ground, Strabo's first task was to clear it of nettles—*summum malum*, the worst enemy of all. 'What *is* one to do?' he asked. 'Deep down the roots are matted and linked and riveted, like basketwork or the wattled hurdles of the fold.' So he seized his 'tooth of Saturn', tore up the clods and laboriously extracted the nettle-roots. Again and again they reappeared, but in the end he was victorious.

In fact, he was faced with just the same sort of problems that you and I are: the awkward corner where there's an overhanging roof; the bit which is starved and shaded by a high brick wall. He hated handling manure, but forced himself to do so for the sake of his plants. He edged his beds with 'stout squared logs', presumably to raise them and thus avoid the necessity of so much stooping. He lists the plants that he grew, and their virtues—recommending, for example, an infusion of horehound 'hot from the fire, after dinner, if you are poisoned by your stepmother'. He writes of sage and southernwood and rue, of gourd and pumpkin, and most rapturously of all of rose and lily: the passage about the lily—'too lovely for the narrow range of my poor muse'—is splendid.

The poem is dedicated to his friend Grimaldus, Abbot of Weissenburg, who is invited to read it and to suggest improvements as he takes his siesta in his orchard, his little pupils playing around him and trying to grasp the enormous apples in their tiny hands.

The poem, so far as I can discover, has only once been done into English—by Richard Lambert, in a very limited edition. His version is in neat but jingling verse—for example:

And the name of the Poppy is said to be due
To the 'pop' of the seeds in your mouth as you chew.

But it really calls for straight prose or the Arthur Waley treatment. I could send you a copy of the text, which runs to about 450 lines. Your Latin is better than mine, and I dare say that I could help a bit with the English; why shouldn't we have a shot at translating it together?

By the way, you asked me what I mean by the 'doctrine of Signatures'. Paracelsus, a sixteenth-century German physician, started the idea that diseases could be cured by treating them with plants, minerals and so on that had some kind of superficial resemblance to the affected parts. For example, the Paracelsians recommended walnuts for diseases of the head because the shell and nut looked like skull and brain. Jaundice was treated with plants that had yellow flowers; bloodstone was supposed to stop a hæmorrhage, and so on. These crazy notions aren't quite dead yet, and I don't doubt that Ovenden believes in them.

Since starting this letter I've been thinking further about artificial flowers, and I begin to wonder whether it might not be best if their makers didn't attempt to imitate real ones. After all, the Creation was rather a rush job—only *one* day for ground clearance *and* the invention of the whole vegetable kingdom. Also, unless Noah took specimen vegetables with him in the Ark, a good many of the prototypes must surely have been lost in the Flood. I think the designers should give us, not just blue daffodils, but possible yet non-existent flowers; that would be really exciting.

Ever your very affectionate godfather

Wilfrid Sharp

P.S. A *most* embarrassing thing has happened. The other day I received by the morning post a letter in Delia's hand, beginning 'Dear Headmaster . . .' Yesterday her most affectionate letter to me was returned to her by the said Headmaster with a very acid accompanying note!

AUGUST

August 3rd

My dearest Flora,

      If you expect me to be *surprised* by your news—well, frankly I am *not*! But I *am* absolutely delighted. You couldn't have found a nicer young man in all Scotland. That Angus was charming was obvious. I thought him far more than that—though of course I only saw him briefly. And you have so many interests in common. I do wish you both every happiness; when are you thinking of getting married?

It seems bathos to turn from this important news to the petty happenings of Dewbury, but perhaps you will like to know what I've been doing. The chief event is that I've permanetly blotted my copybook with Mrs. Puttenham—and it really wasn't my fault. You shall judge for yourself.

Oliver has been here several afternoons this week helping me to clear that large clump of overgrown laurels at the end of the drive. Yesterday I had to go off to have tea with Helen, so I told him he could stay on a bit if he liked and play the gramophone. I came back at seven and found him still there; he was slumped in my armchair and looking very flushed, and the gramophone was grating round in the last groove. 'I think I'm a bit squiffy,' he said. He staggered to his feet and was immediately sick. He'd got at my gin and drunk—at a guess—a good quarter of a bottle of it!

Mrs. Benham came to the rescue of what she called 'the poor child'; 'bloody little fool' was what I'd called him a few moments earlier. We sobered him down as best we could and then I took him home in my car. Fortunately his mother was out, so I handed him over to the housekeeper and had a talk with her about him. She told me what I hadn't known before—that he'd been sacked from Harrow for keeping gin in his room and being found completely tight. 'My lady gave him so much pocket-money. Of course they can't really sell it to a boy, but you can do anything if you've got money. My lady has to keep all the spirits locked up. It's a shame; he's a nice boy really. You won't tell my lady I told you all this, will you?' I said I wouldn't. But I did wish I'd known it sooner; he'd have told me himself if I hadn't choked him off. I then remembered Delia telling me, at her party, to see that he only had sherry; she said she didn't know why he'd had to leave Harrow, but she may have had a pretty shrewd idea. I wish she'd given me a hint.

I tried to convey to the housekeeper that I thought Oliver had learned his lesson and that I didn't consider anything was to be gained by mentioning the matter to

Mrs. P.; I'd have told any reasonable parent under the circumstances. Perhaps I was wrong; anyhow it didn't work, and one of her gardeners has just delivered an extremely offensive letter from her. She says that she has told Oliver that he isn't to come to Orchards in future. This is a pity, because I like having him here and I'm sure I'm a help to him. I've now written her a much nicer letter than she deserves, telling her exactly what happened. The whole thing is extremely tiresome.

Bose again!—Bose on the mimosa. He found that it went through 'a daily cycle of sensibility and insensibility which may be aptly described as waking and sleeping'. He discovered that mimosa was 'a late riser', stirring around 9 a.m. and gradually rousing itself in quite a human way. It grew 'somewhat sleepy between 9 p.m. and 2 a.m. but was still awake at 6 a.m., after which it fell sound asleep and remained so until past 8 a.m. . . . Apparently mimosa has forestalled the dissipated life of the modern Babylons of London, Paris and New York, staying up all night and going to bed only after the rising of the sun!'

And Bose on waterlilies. Why, he wondered, did the Indian waterlily close by day and open by night, whereas European waterlilies opened by day and closed by night. He soon discovered that light and darkness had little or nothing to do with it; it was a matter of heat and cold, which didn't exactly correspond with day and night. Then he found the answer: in the Indian waterlily the outer side of the petals was more sensitive to a change of temperature than the inner, whereas in the

European it was the reverse. Therefore heat opened the petals of the European lilies, but closed those of the Indian. Isn't that fascinating?

While we're on waterlilies, do you know Abraham Cowley's poem on the subject, beginning:

> Dy'e slight me, 'cause a bog my Belly feeds,
> And I am found among a crowd of Reeds?
> I'm no green vulgar Daughter of the Earth,
> But to the noble Waters owe my birth . . .

Cowley's flower-poems are slightly absurd but great fun. Some of them are addressed to the most unpromising plants: scurvy-grass, dodder, lustwort, ducks-meat, miltwast ('Me cruel Nature, when she made me, gave / Nor stalk, nor seed, nor flow'r, as others have') and lettuce ('Eat me with Bread and Oil, you'll ne'r repine'). There are no less than four poems to the sowbread (cyclamen), one of which is this rather coarse but amusing epigram:

> The dropping, bloudy Nose you gently bind,
> But loosen the close Hemorrhoids behind.
> And 'tis but natural, that who shuts the Fore
> Shou'd at the same time open the back-door.

I've just discovered, with much satisfaction, that Herbert Spencer had artificial flowers, bought and carefully arranged by himself, in his drawing-room. To a friend who said (in a tone of unutterable disgust), 'Whoever would suppose that Herbert Spencer would have anything but real flowers in his house!' Spencer replied, 'Pooh! real flowers would want constant replenishing.' And pointing to a landscape painting he added, 'Why in the world, now, do you object to artificial flowers in a room any more than to an artificial landscape?'

By the way, I'm not writing separately to Angus, so will you please pass my congratulations on to him. Also I quite see that you'll now have more important things to do than translating Strabo!

August 10th

It has been a notable week: cobaea and the moon-flower have both opened! First the cobaea. About ten days ago the flanged bud, which had been upturned, began to tilt forwards and the pale-green petals, tightly clasped together, to emerge from the calyx. The flower then looked rather like a very self-conscious large green acorn in a crinkly cup. Soon the petals began to work apart until a small circular opening formed at the tip; it now seemed to make a moue like a mouth spitting out a cherry-stone. Gradually the mouth opened wider, exposing a stockade of anthers that grinned like golden-green teeth.

When it had opened fully, the flower had the cup-and-saucer shape of a Canterbury bell, but with the style and filaments lying flat against the lowest part of it like a tongue saying 'Ah!' to a doctor. Next day the lime-green became flushed with pink which gradually turned to a rich purple. Then this morning—the fourth day—the flower suddenly dropped entire to the ground, where it stood like a small purple volcano. Now there are quantities more buds coming along, and I believe it ought to stay in flower until Christmas.

And, not to be outdone, the first moonflower came out last night! The bud, like a white furled umbrella with apple-green ribs, opened at about 7 o'clock, and I was present at the birth. It really is a glorious thing; but I can't understand why Count de Mauny talked of a *cream*-coloured *cup*: it's a silvery-white plate on a long white tube, silken in texture and deliciously scented. I carried it in triumph to Mrs. Benham and thence to my dinner-table. It saw me through the evening; this morning it was dead.

Noticing with my dissecting microscope (did I tell you I'd got one?) that each stamen of my cobaea is embedded in a felty tuft of hairs, presumably placed there to keep the wrong kind of insects from getting at the honey, I started reading about what Kerner calls 'the reception of flower-seeking animals at the flower'. (Did you know that the association between flowers and insects was at least forty million years old?)

Some visitors are always unwelcome—those that would take the honey without fertilizing the flower. Others are welcome—if they arrive at the right time and behave correctly. The flower takes steps to discourage over-punctual and belated guests. The former merely find the doors not yet open; the latter are warned in various ways that the service is discontinued. Some flowers 'drop': that's to say, take down the notice-board. Others draw their petals together again—for example the yucca, whose buds and dead flowers you can hardly tell apart. Yet others hang their heads, draw a barrier across the threshold, or change to a colour that doesn't attract.

But when—I was almost going to say, 'when lunch is being served,' but I must resist—when the right moment arrives, the flowers lay themselves out to make their guests comfortable. The foxglove adjusts the angle of its head and sticks out its lower lip to serve as a landing-stage. Each individual flower of the laburnum, when the whole tassel bends downwards, twists itself round just before it opens and so makes an alighting-platform of its keel. The snapdragon only opens its door when a visitor as ponderous and as welcome as a bumble-bee settles on the bloated lower lip. Flowers fertilized by moths (such as honeysuckle) or humming-birds need no platform and usually have none; but the Chilean puyas, if it is true that they are fertilized by humming-birds, are exceptions, for they have (and I wonder why) most elaborate perches.

In general, flowers want to discourage little insects

from climbing up their stems to the flower-heads, for these are simply robbers. The Himalayan balsam has a neat trick: as its flower opens, the plant manufactures a drop of honey at the base of every leaf. This satisfies the ants, which climb no further. With the Banksian rose (and some others also) the ants are actually co-operative; when the leaves are attacked by leaf-eating insects, the ants declare war on them, biting them and squirting them with formic acid. Water-plants are of course protected by the water that surrounds them; but the teasel makes its own moat at the base of its leaves.

There are other devices too—sticky secretions on flower or leaf, waxed inclines too slippery to climb, tufts and palisades of hairs and bristles. Against snails and caterpillars, which are not honey-seekers but ruthless destroyers, the prickly calyx is good protection. Then why, if Nature *can* do all this, doesn't she protect my sweet Williams from slugs, my petunias from snails? Kerner has a passage which is suggestive. There are certain flowers (some 300 in Europe alone) which bumble-bees rob of their honey by biting a hole in the calyx. These plants, he says, date back to a time when the bumble-bee didn't frequent the regions where they grow; and now, for lack of fertilization, they are dying out. I can only suppose my petunias and sweet Williams come from lands where, once at any rate, there were no snails and no slugs.

Delia has a Swiss boy staying with her, who is over here to learn the language. He has been dumped on her for a fortnight by a friend of a friend: Delia's

R

warm-heartedness is always landing her in situations of this kind. She rang me up. 'Darling! Klaus is perfectly *sweet*, but he's only got school English and it isn't very good. He's German-Swiss, and *you* speak German, don't you? I suppose you wouldn't be an absolute *angel* and take him over to Wisley tomorrow when I have to be in London? He's mad about flowers.'

Of course I agreed. 'At least he's not likely to be as hard work as Mrs. Anderson,' I said.

But he was! 'I—I *lernte*—vot can I zay? "learned"? I zank you—I learned in ze—vot can I say, *Schule*? "school"? I zank you. But now I do not come to talk. I am not a maiden. Am I a maiden?'

'I shouldn't have thought so.'

'You—you *verstehen*—vot can I zay? "understand"? I zank you. You understand?'

'I'm afraid I don't quite follow.'

'Follow? I do not understand.'

'I mean, I don't quite understand about your not being a girl.'

'A girl? I do not understand.'

'A maiden.'

'I understand. You do not understand?'

I didn't. I still haven't the faintest idea what he was trying to tell me. He did look rather like a large pink heifer, but he can hardly have meant that. He wasn't in the least interested in flowers (where we might have talked Latin); and he stubbornly refused to speak a word of German. I felt pretty mad with Delia for landing him on me for four hours; but when I remembered that she was in for a fortnight of him, my anger turned to deepest sympathy.

There's been a little storm in the Dewbury teacup. Mrs. Puttenham met Susanna in her magenta jeans (which really *don't* suit her) and told her that they were letting down the tone of the village. Susanna lost her temper, said that what she was wearing was, as near as made no odds, Armenian native costume, and added—somewhat illogically—that Mrs. P. would be greeted with howls of derision if she appeared in Mush in a hat like that. Then she bowled away before the squiress had sufficiently recovered from shock to answer. The scene was witnessed by Peters as he was dusting his gnome; his account of it more or less tallied with Susanna's, though Susanna's was more colourful and less coherent.

Dewburians, though they don't much care for Susanna's jeans, are behind her to a man—and especially, to a woman. Helen declares that she'll never play another accompaniment for Mrs. Puttenham. Delia (now back from Scotland) is said to be ordering a pair of magenta jeans to wear at the Conservative fête at the Manor, and Humphrey to have announced that if she does he'll institute divorce proceedings.

By the way, Delia tells me that you pointed out Angus to her and that though she didn't speak to him she decided that he looked 'a perfect *angel*'. She sends you her love; I'm sure she will have written to you.

P.S. Do you know if there was a year 'o', or did it jump from I B.C. to A.D. I?

August 17th

The day after I had taken Klaus to Wisley, Delia rang me up. 'Darling, I *can't* thank you enough! When I got in I found Klaus simply *ecstatic*. He *adored* the flowers, *and* the drive, *and* the tea, and *you* and—well, *everything*. You know, darling, you really *have* got a little something.

I said, 'Come off it, Delia! It was a ghastly flop—the whole thing. Klaus understood nothing I said, I understood nothing he said. He was bored stiff by the flowers, *and* by me. I grant you he seemed to enjoy the tea, and even Susanna couldn't have got through more in the time. How did he convey to you all this ecstasy? By ballet gestures or yodelling or how? You're not going to make me believe you can understand his English; he has a vocabulary of seven words, five of which are more or less incomprehensible as he pronounces them.'

Delia said, 'Darling, *I could see it in his eyes.* The trouble with *you*, darling, is that you're too *modest.* Actually, I was going to ask *another* favour of you—and now I hardly dare. . . . I *need* you—on Monday! Mrs. Leggett—I hear you met her at Mrs. Trehearne's silver wedding—has invited herself to luncheon with *all* her daughters—Charity is one of my fifty-three godchildren —and Humphrey won't be there and Klaus will have gone and I *can't* face them alone. Will you be an *angel* . . .?' As you know, I consider Delia's slightest wish a command.

The Misses Leggett—Faith, Hope, Charity and Prudence—are all about six foot, thin as pea-sticks and acid as acid drops. F., H. and C. are triplets, middle or late thirties, and P. a considerable afterthought ('Darling! Perhaps she ought really to have been called "*Im*prudence"'). Mrs. Leggett announced at lunch that men these days weren't men at all—which I took to mean that none of them had proposed to a Miss Leggett. She added that women weren't women either—she'd seen an unspeakable sight in the village: a fat black Jewess in purple tights. Delia said, 'Darling! You ought to meet Mrs. Puttenham.' They left at 4 o'clock, laden with flowers, chocolates and home-made cream cheese and a good deal less grateful, I thought, than circumstances warranted.

After they'd gone I said to Delia, 'I can't imagine why you asked them.' 'But, Darling! I *didn't*: they asked themselves. Those poor girls don't get much fun. You were perfectly *sweet* to them and they're all *madly* in love with you. Darling! Oughtn't you to marry Charity? She's a very good cook and she'd soon fatten up. And she's just the right age. You know what Aristotle (*was* it Aristotle?) said: half the man's age plus seven. Charity's thirty-seven I believe, so it's exactly right.' I told her that in such matters charity began at home.

Yes, of course you're perfectly right about Kerner; it's seventy years old now, and no doubt a lot of stuff in it is out of date. And I expect it's the same with Bose; Patrick Synge tells me that various botanists have tried to repeat his experiments, but that none of them has got the same kind of results. Are you getting too much of Bose, for if you are I'll stop?

But the point is this. While I was in the City I had little time for reading. And I've never had any botanical training. If anyone can recommend me a modern book that covers the same ground that Kerner does, as fully and clearly and with such excellent illustrations—then I'll gladly throw my Kerner into the dustbin. But I can't find anything that gives a comparable picture of plant life. I *know* I ought to understand more about chromosomes and tetraploids. Not knowing about chromosomes nowadays is as bad as not knowing about Boulez or Francis Bacon or Thom Gunn: it puts one outside the pale. But I can't help it; I date from the pre-chromosome age. Eric did lend me a book on the subject—I forget the author's name—which he claimed a child of nine could understand. All I can say is that I couldn't. But before returning it to him I copied out this passage:

'There are, for instance, 12 chromosomes in Broad Bean, 16 in Crocus, 24 in Lily and Tulip, 32 in Cherry, 34 in the Yellow Flag Iris, 48 in Tobacco— the same number, incidentally, as in man.' No doubt that's why I smoke so much.

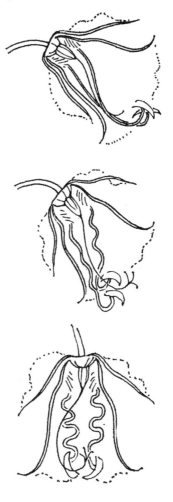

I've been studying (with old Kerner's help) the fertilization of the cobaea; I'll try to draw for you, diagrammatically, what happens. When the flower first opens the style is short, its tip tucked under the stamens. Then the flower nods, the style grows longer and divides into three at the tip, and the filaments corkscrew and withdraw; all is now ready for an insect to bring pollen from a younger flower. But—and this is what is so ingenious—if no insect arrives, the flower becomes completely pendant and, by further acrobatics and contortions, fertilizes itself! This, you may care to know, is called 'autogamy'.

Seeing the cobaea fall so neatly and entire to the ground set me thinking about the different ways in which flowers die. One could tell sad stories of the death of flowers, some of which die very disagreeably, though Caroline Bowles envies them all:

How happily, how happily the flowers die away!
Oh, could we but return to earth as easily as they!
Just live a life of sunshine, of innocence and bloom,
Then drop without decrepitude or pain into the tomb.

But first there is their life-span. The morning glory lasts less than a single day, and there is a tropical hibiscus which comes and goes in three or four hours. Yet there are tropical orchids whose individual flowers remain perfect for six or seven weeks.

A certain Miss Cobbe once wrote, said Ruskin, that 'all wild flowers know how to die gracefully'. He doesn't say whether or not he agreed; I don't. The wild daffodil sickens and dies as nastily as the garden varieties, lingering moribund among the living, a shrivelled and evil-smelling *memento mori*. The best deaths, as for man, are those that are sudden—and, when I think of the tortured look of a dying daffodil I feel I might almost add (and I'm sure Bose would agree), painless. The cobaea, like the foxglove or the camellia, is one moment living, the next dead; it's as though some hidden catch were suddenly released—and I dare say it is. The poppy drops petal by petal but cleanly (hence the *rhoeas*, meaning 'flowing', of the corn-poppy), leaving behind the memorial of its fine capsule. But most flowers die slowly, browning and writhing and reeking into shrunken mummies, mere caricatures of what they once had been. May we all die like cobaea!

There are people who have no use for painters and poets and musicians until they are dead. But I once had a friend who only liked dead *flowers*! It was very convenient: I would wait until I could bear those daffodils on my table no longer, then take them round as a most acceptable gift.

P.S. I really think it *must* be a catch that controls the cobaea. Seeing a flower that was obviously nearing the end of its lifespan, I gave it a sharp tug: it didn't yield. But an hour later I found it had fallen. I wish I could understand how such things happen; no book ever seems to tell one—not, at least, in language the layman can follow.

August 24th

You may perhaps know about this already, because
the *Telegraph* and the *Express* both got hold of it; but
the *Richmond and Twickenham Courier*, which you won't
have seen, has a fuller account. What a miserable thing
it all is! Eric's behaviour in Court was quite impossible;
I really think he must be a little mad. It's Pamela I'm
sorry for:

THEFTS FROM KEW GARDENS
SURREY GARDENER IN COURT

Eric Leighton, aged 51, of Ashton's Bottom, Din-
ton, appeared at the West London Court on Wednesday on a charge of stealing plants from the Royal
Botanic Gardens, Kew. He pleaded not guilty, and
conducted his own defence.

Mr. Humbolt, an official of the Royal Botanic
Gardens, said in evidence that as a result of recent
thefts from the rock garden a special watch had been
kept. The accused was seen to approach a small
group of liliaceous plants. After satisfying himself
that he was not observed, he took a trowel from his
coat pocket and dug up two bulbs. . . .

Mr. Evans (prosecuting): 'I understand that these
were rare plants?'

Mr. Humbolt: 'Yes, Sir. Very rare indeed.'

Mr. Evans: 'Then why were they not kept in a
greenhouse?'

Mr. Humbolt: 'Because they would have died
there.'

Mr. Evans: 'Please continue.'

Mr. Humbolt: 'On being questioned by one of the guardians, the accused admitted taking the bulbs, but maintained that as he had often donated plants to the Gardens he considered himself entitled to do so. Three other plants and various cuttings were found on his person.'

Mr. Evans: 'What is a cutting?'

Mr. Humbolt: 'A cutting is a small shoot or branch removed from the parent plant for the purpose of propagation. Whereas propagation by seed may not come true, plants propagated vegetatively, that is to say by means of cuttings or by division of . . .

The Magistrate (to the accused): 'Do you admit taking these bulbs and cuttings? And if so, how do you attempt to justify your action? Have you anything to say?'

Leighton: 'I have indeed; a very great deal. As a regular donor to the Gardens, and as a rate-payer, I consider myself perfectly entitled to take plants and cuttings when I do so without damaging or unreasonably reducing the size of the plant. I am not the kind of man who would take the single egg from a nest. I consider that rare plants should be as widely distributed as . . .'

The Magistrate (interrupting—to Mr. Humbolt): 'Has the accused given plants to the Gardens?'

Mr. Humbolt: 'Yes, Sir. On a number of occasions.'

The Magistrate (to Leighton): 'Whether or no

you have from time to time presented plants to the Gardens, what you have committed is theft. Are you sorry for what you have done?'

Leighton: 'Not in the least. And I shall do it again.'

The Magistrate: 'Are you aware that I have power to commit you to prison? Will you express regret for your very foolish action?'

Leighton: 'No—I will not.'

The Magistrate: 'Very well, then. I find you guilty and you will have to pay a fine of £20.'

Leighton: 'I shan't pay.'

The Magistrate: 'You may have seven days to pay. If you do not pay, then you will have to go to prison for two months.'

Leighton: 'I haven't the slightest intention of paying.'

The accused left the court. It was learned later that his wife had paid the fine.

What makes it so unfortunate is that Eric *is* so generous with his plants. Yet obviously the guardian who caught him and summoned a policeman couldn't know this, and in any case could hardly have acted otherwise; and once the machinery had been set in motion it was inevitable that there should be a prosecution. There seems very little doubt that if Eric had behaved sensibly in court he would have got off, under the First Offenders' Act, with a caution.

I've been having a further look at cobaea through my

lenses. The texture of the flower before it opens is curious: it looks as if it were made of lime-green papier mâché pressed in a crinkly mould. But once open it becomes translucent. Each filament is nearly two inches long, and like a shepherd's crook made of yellow-green jade. Where the anther is attached—the point where you'd suppose most strength was needed—the filament tapers away into a fine white thread. Each anther is a good half-inch in length and formed like a canoe with a 'nick' at one end; it's straw-coloured, with two claret-coloured stripes inside and two more outside—a lovely thing.

The sepals are also well worth studying. They are crinkled like holly-leaves (but not spiked), and a fresh lettuce-green with a network of white veining. Through the low-power lens they look like an aerial view of pastoral country intersected by main roads and side roads.

The pollen grains are about 1/120 inch in diameter, and spherical—which is unusual; pollen grains are generally ellipsoidal. With my × 20 lens I could just see that the surface of them was lightly honeycombed: in fact, they look like miniature golf-balls. The purpose of the honeycombing would seem to be to prevent water reaching the pollen cells too soon, each little cavity retaining a pocket of air which delays the entry of moisture. Ultimately the cells do need moisture, and in time it forces its way through the ribs.

Delia, when I was in her garden yesterday, said, 'Don't you think the smell of night-scented stock is one of the best of all? I wonder why it's called *Matthiola tristis*; it *can't* be unhappy if it smells like that.' 'Yes,' I agreed. 'The stock (to quote Mr. Robert Gathorne-Hardy) has indeed "the pleasant attribute of nocturnal fragrance". Did you know that it's so sensitive that it will actually open during an eclipse of the sun?' It was a lovely warm evening; the air was full of it, and it seemed to follow me all the way home. So over my dinner, and after, I read the subject up.

'Odorous flowers,' says Mr. Knight, 'are of two kinds, fragrant and foetid': in other words, some flowers smell good, some bad, some not at all. How wretchedly meagre and unsatisfactory is our vocabulary of 'smell'! As Vita Sackville-West wrote, ' "Smells good" is an honest phrase at least, and neither "scent" nor "perfume" nor "odour" nor "fragrance" can take its place' —nor, indeed, 'aroma'; and she leaves these 'genteel substitutions' to those writers on flowers who indulge in words such as 'quaint', 'dainty' and 'winsome'.

It isn't easy to put smells into categories, though of course attempts have been made: the hawthorn type, the carnation type, and so on. There are the pervasive smells, such as that of lime, which are stronger at a certain distance away from the flower. In fact, Bacon would claim this property for all flowers: 'The breath of flowers is far sweeter in the air (where it comes and goes like the warbling of music) than in the hand.' There are smells that are not for everyone: of dying strawberry leaves, 'cordial to those to whose olfactory nerves it is gratefully evident'; of Exaltolide (a synthetic scent), which only women can smell. There is taste in smells: some people do, and some don't, like the smell of peonies. René Rapin, the seventeenth-century Jesuit author of *The Garden*, didn't; the peony's blushes, he wrote, might seem to suggest virtue, 'But her vile Scent betrays they rise from Shame'. (Which reminds me that I once saw, in America, a poster advertisement showing a blushing peony standing between two leering white lilies and captioned, 'SOMEBODY ISN'T USING ——').

Smells serve to attract, or to repel, animals. The smell of the leaves of garlic discourages browsing animals, the smell of its flowers attracts the desired insects. If you mutilate the flower of a fly orchid until it's unrecogniz-able, but leave the part that produces the smell, the par-ticular wasps that fertilize it will still visit it. A German named Kroll, using a set of wild arums made wholly or partly of glass, some with the spadix smeared with excrement and others not, proved that it wasn't the colour or the warmth, but only the stench, that attracted the various dung-loving flies and beetles that the wild arum needs.

What are *your* 'best-smellers'? I think I put gardenia top—but partly, I admit, for sentimental reasons. Lily of the valley, *Daphne odora*, hyacinth; jasmine, clove carnation—it's impossible to choose the 'best six'. And the 'worst six'? There is a Mediterranean orchid that reeks of goats, an American parasite of putrid fish, an aristolochia of stale tobacco. *Calycanthus floridus* smells of fermenting wine, and some of the stapelias (so I'm assured) of sailors' trousers. Most bad-smelling flowers are the colour of raw meat or the corpses of animals; they're reddish, greenish, fawn, with violet flecks and livid streaks; and many smell of excrement. The dragon arum is a shocker; but in my opinion the sickly fetor of the common stink-horn fungus beats the lot—you can sometimes smell it a hundred yards or more away.

Oliver has been round this morning, in defiance of the interdict, bringing me half-a-dozen bulbs of *Lilium testaceum* that he'd bought out of his pocket-money. (Incidentally he's had half his hair cut off in Dorking 'to annoy Mother'.) 'It really ought to have been gin,' he said. 'I tried to get Chandler to buy me some, but he wouldn't. Mother's told me not to come here any more, but I wanted to say I was sorry. Mother says you made me drunk, and I told her it was a lie. But she's telling everybody all the same.'

I felt I had to have it out with him. I got him to tell me—which he did at once—why he'd had to leave Harrow, and much though I hate being pompous I said what I felt needed saying. I told him too that since his mother had forbidden him to come and see me, then—though of course I'd regret it—he mustn't come; but that when I got the chance I'd talk to her about it. He asked if he could play the Siegfried Idyll, so I gave him my record to take home with him.

It's splendid that you've found a house. Of course it can't be *exactly* what you were looking for, but at least it's got some sort of garden. I must put you in touch with Peter Davis at the Edinburgh Botanic Garden— he's an old friend of mine (we once botanized together in Morocco in my bachelor days) and I'm sure you'll find him helpful.

P.S. Do you happen to know anything about 'the Maid of Germany', mentioned by Sir Thomas Browne, who 'lived without meat on the smell of a rose'? I can't track her down.

August 30th   St. Fiacre's Day

I bet you didn't know that St. Fiacre was the patron saint of gardening! What's more, he was probably a Scot (or failing that, an Irishman), who thirteen hundred years ago went to northern France to convert the Gauls—not to gardening (to which they have never been properly converted), but to Christianity. He is only indirectly related to the cab: the first cabs were, it seems, kept at the *auberge* of St. Fiacre in Paris. There's another gardening saint—St. Phocas; but he was a

S

poor-spirited creature who, sighing after martyrdom, quite gratuitously betrayed himself and then *asked* to be executed. Being handy with a spade, he even voluntarily dug his own grave beforehand—to save time and trouble. Let us rather pray to St. Fiacre.

I brought back yesterday, from the Royal Horticultural Society's Library, a little book called *Flower Scent*, by F. A. Hampton; it so absorbed me that I didn't realize I'd reached the Dorking Coach Station until the conductor came up and asked me if I intended going back to London again. I can't do more than tell you a few stray things in it that amused me. For example, that hawthorn smells slightly fishy—for the very good reason that its flowers contain *trimethylamine*, a substance found in large quantities in herring brine. Here are one or two of the more curious plant smells given by Hampton:

St. John's wort: 'Apples and goats'.

Citriosma oligandra: 'Bergamot and goats—which is said to suggest the characteristic smell of the Negro and is known in Brazil as "Catinga de Nigra".' (*Catinga* is the Portuguese for B.O.) But its name suggests that it should smell of lemon.

Crown Imperial (bulbs): 'Foxes'.

Dendrobium devonianum (a tropical orchid): 'has a distinctly human scent mixed with its sweetness, and is said to recall a dance room on a warm evening'.

Rosa lutea: 'Bugs and raspberries'.

Crocus graveolens: 'Blackbeetles'.

Some flowers smell differently at different times—for instance, our native pyramidal orchis 'is sweetly scented by day, but gives off a foxy smell at night'. Some have what the Germans call a 'Nachgeruch'—an 'after-smell': the sweetness of the garden phlox 'is clearly related to that of the double stocks, but it has in the background a strong smell recalling at first walnuts and then a clean pigsty'. Some smells are pleasant when dilute but disagreeable when concentrated. Two sweet scents, indol and scatol,

> at a very high dilution have a pleasant flowery scent, recalling Jonquil; when slightly stronger an element suggesting old clothes and sable fur comes in, which rapidly passes, with increasing concentration, into the smell of the lion house at the Zoo, and then into a frank stench. . . . Miss Jekyll records that the scent of a bunch of Jasmine on a hot night in Jamaica gave rise to the suspicion of a dead rat under the floor, which is quite a logical association of seeming opposites, since indol is present in both.

Many animals are of course attracted by the smell of flowers. 'Cats are passionately fond of [*Micromeria corsica*], rolling on it with expressions of ecstatic delight and often destroying it in the rock garden.' Bees 'perceive the same smells that we do, and with about the same acuity; they also fail to discriminate between those scents which we ourselves find difficult to distinguish'. But, unlike moths and butterflies, they are more attracted by the colour of flowers than by their smell.

I'd never realized that many butterflies smell good, and that this smell was made use of in their 'courtship'; but whereas it's the female of the human species that uses scent to captivate the male, it's the male butterfly that is provided with scent organs. Hampton prefers the word 'courtship' to 'mating' because 'a sweet scent is one that can stir the instinct of courtship without evoking the idea of the natural end object of the instinct'. He adds that 'since the flower has been evolved entirely in relation with the insects that visit it, we must conclude that had it not been for the scent of butterflies we should have had no fragrant flowers'. Butterflies are not the only animals that smell. Old Sir Thomas Browne wrote, 'we find so noble a scent in the Tulip Fly and the Goat Beetle', and among mammals there is the whole gamut of smells from the skunk to Walt Whitman, who smelt of violets, and H. G. Wells, who smelt of honey.

Hampton has a good chapter on how scent is made. Labdanum used to be collected in Cyprus by driving flocks of sheep among the cistus bushes and then combing the resin out of the fleeces. The distillation processes are complicated, and I didn't feel like following up his recipe for manufacturing scent in the home, which involves the purchase of large quantities of beef suet and three months of regular bottle-shaking in a dark cupboard.

But enough of Hampton. Pamela Leighton came to see me on Thursday. She burst into tears and told me everything—how she'd been bullied and neglected for twenty years. But the worst was that, a month ago, she'd finally made up her mind to leave Eric—and now, of course, she can't: people would say she'd deserted him when he was in trouble.

She kept looking at her watch. 'I told Eric I was going to do some shopping in Dorking,' she said. 'He'll be wondering why I'm not back.' I comforted her as best I could and told her she could come and talk to me whenever she liked—if it helped at all. Then, without thinking, I picked her a few roses. But she thrust them back at me: 'How can I? Eric would know where I'd been!'

Poor woman!

Mrs. Puttenham has told Helen that I'm a corrupter of youth and have been systematically turning Oliver into an alcoholic. This is rather hard—and probably actionable. He's not been round again, but Susanna's attentions have been redoubled; she's absolutely vitriolic on the subject of Mrs. P.

Cobaea has grown to a height of fifteen feet, but it's beginning to show its Achilles' heels. The lower leaves are getting tatty, and then last night a high wind brought the top seven or eight feet off the wall. Those little tendrils are too frail for the English climate. However, the stem is so rubbery that it hasn't snapped; it merely looks very woebegone, and I've rehoused it as best I could on a lower level.

Looking at the cobaea through my lens the other day set me thinking about the texture of flowers and leaves; the velvet of the gloxinia, the satin of the petunia, the ruby glass of the poppy, the sheer taffeta of the black pansy: what gives to each its particular quality!

The gloxinia looks like velvet because it *is* velvet: from the surface of the petals uprise a great army of tiny, short, almost vertical hairs that correspond exactly to the pile of velvet. The silk of the leaf of *Convolvulus cneorum* is produced by long hairs lying against the leaf and reflecting the light. The hairs of plants that look 'woollen' are twisted and tangled. Hairs like little fir-trees give *Verbascum thapsiforme* the quality of flock. But it's maddening that my dissecting microscope isn't quite strong enough to show all I want to see, and some of the flowers I'd like to look at are already over.

Your mother and father have been here, and I got through a whole afternoon without crossing swords with your mother. Your father looked wonderfully better; I believe your engagement is the principal cause—he's absolutely delighted about it, and so too is your mother.

Ever your very affectionate godfather

Wilfrid Sharp

P.S. From an obituary notice: 'Mr. Moggridge was no mere dilettante naturalist, who confined himself to unintelligent admiration of the works of the Creator . . .' Comment unnecessary!

SEPTEMBER

September 8th

My dearest Flora,

This morning I woke to autumn—a warm autumn morning rather than the cool summer morning of yesterday. It's like the difference between a fiddle and a 'cello both playing middle C: the same note, but another quality. There was a light veil of mist on the meadow, dew heavy on the rough grass where the colchicums are in flower; and nearby in the shorter grass the first autumn crocuses were showing. I grow a bit bored with my garden as August ebbs, but the colchicums and crocuses always rouse me. The waning of the year is melancholy, but the crocuses are like spring at one's feet.

I'm sending you off this morning a dozen figs from my tree, which is bearing very well this year; I hope they'll arrive in good condition. Have you ever read Samuel Butler's *The Way of All Flesh*? If so, you may remember Ernest Pontifex's sermon on the barren fig-tree in which he described 'the hopes of the owner as he watched the delicate blossom unfold, and give promise of such beautiful fruit in autumn', only to be told afterwards by a botanical member of his congregation that this was unlikely because, roughly speaking, the fig produces its fruit first and blossoms inside the fruit.

Writers also are often pretty careless over scientific accuracy. Drayton's nymph composed a garland of mixed flowers which couldn't possibly have been picked at the same time. Shelley can hardly have watched all day 'the yellow bees in the ivy bloom', nor can Gray (as Lord David Cecil alleges) have picked bog asphodel on the banks of the Thames while a boy at Eton. Virginia Woolf, in *Orlando*, has 'the dahlia in all its varieties' in full flower in Europe in the seventeenth century; and even the great Sir Edward Salisbury, as the result of confusing *formosa* ('beautiful') with *formosana* ('from Formosa'), wrote of the Himalayan *Leycesteria formosa* that it added a 'Japanese' element to our shrubberies. Look at almost any technicolour film of, say, imperial Rome, and you are sure to see some pretty unexpected flowers in the atrium.

But to return to the fig: did you in fact realize that when you ate a fig you were actually eating a bunch of flowers growing inside the 'fruit'? Look when you cut one open. There are ordinary male and female flowers, and a special kind of female flower in which a special kind of wasp deposits its eggs and converts it into a gall. The story of the fertilization of figs by these wasps is a most extraordinary one, but so complicated that it must wait till a later occasion.

It was Reginald (afterwards Cardinal) Pole who brought the first fig-trees back from Italy and had them planted in the Palace gardens at Lambeth in 1525. There are, of course, lots of other figs—about 600 of them—besides those we eat, and they're a pretty mixed bag. There's the banyan with its hundreds of aerial roots that make a sort of columned hall like the Mosque at Cordoba; Gerard has a nice picture of it, and mentions the 'admirable eccho that doth resound or answer again fower or fiue times'. There is *Ficus religiosa*—the Bo-tree or Pepul—under whose branches the Buddha is said to have learned the secret of the universe. But the fig one sees most often nowadays is *F. elastica*, the Rubber Plant, which seems to have been specially designed to make the best of contemporary furniture and central heating.

If you turn to Isaiah xxxviii, v. 21, you can read about Hezekiah's boil which was cured by 'a lump of figs' prescribed by Isaiah—the first poultice in history. And I like the following, from Lady Callcott's *Scripture Herbal* (1842): 'It has been sharply disputed whether the leaves of the common Fig were really those which formed the covering of our first parents. . . . But the dispute is frivolous, since, whatever leaves they might be, they were gathered from the trees of Paradise, and far beyond our search.' I believe that a German professor has written a portentous volume on *Das Feigenblatt in der Kunst*, and doubtless identified the Biblical fig beyond dispute.

Do you know the origin of the word 'sycophant'? The

first meaning was 'an informer' and it comes from the Greek words for 'fig' and 'to declare'. Sycophants were those who sneaked upon people who smuggled figs out of Attica—which was illegal. At least, that's what the smaller dictionaries say: bigger ones hint—as big dictionaries often do—at something very indelicate.

Anyhow, we have Micah's promise that when we have beaten our swords into ploughshares we shall each of us sit under his own fig-tree—and I hope mine won't turn out to be barren.

I've got further evidence that Mrs. Puttenham is blackening my name in the neighbourhood, and I'm not going to stand for it much longer. I miss Oliver's visits. I ran into him yesterday in the village and he begged to be allowed to come and see me. I promised I'd go and have a talk with his mother.

P.S. Delia said yesterday, 'Wild flowers should never be arranged by anyone over the age of five.' I know exactly what she means.

September 16th

Fancy your walking nearly a mile! It's absolutely tremendous; I doubt whether I could do it myself any longer. I think it's about time you left that Angus McGrath of yours for a bit and came south to see the rest of us. Now that your father is so much better, your last excuse vanishes.

No—I don't see any objection to a November wedding, particularly if you decide to go to Madeira and the Canaries for your honeymoon. I remember we bathed at Orotava on New Year's Day and the sea was quite warm. If you do, look out for *Pancratium canariense*, which is lovely and grows all over the cliffs—I brought it back but could never get it to flower. There were some splendid echiums on Teide—which is what they call Mt. Teneriffe. I climbed to the top: however did I do it?

I am sending you a cheque as a wedding present, and hope it may help you to get a few things for the new house. It's really simpler and more satisfactory that way, and then you can choose what you like. It goes to you with all my love and best wishes for your future happiness.

Now local news. Having decided that I'd had about enough of Mrs. Puttenham's slanders, I wrote to her saying that I proposed calling on her at 6 o'clock the following evening. Needless to say, she kept me waiting, so I had time to examine the enormous set-pieces of flowers arranged by Chandler. I guarantee that if the crudest paper imitations were substituted, and left un-changed and undusted for a year, she'd never notice.

She sailed into the room, looking every inch the *Hon.* Mrs. Puttenham, and asked rather acidly what she could do for me. That got my goat: 'The first thing you can do,' I said, 'is to stop slandering me in the village.' She isn't used to being talked to like that, and tried to interrupt me; but I cut her short. I told her, all over again, the facts of Oliver's unfortunate lapse, and men-tioned that since he'd been removed from Harrow for gin-drinking before I'd even met him, she could hardly claim that I'd taught him to drink. This was a shock to her: she didn't know I knew. I expect she was also wondering if I knew (I didn't; Helen only told me today) that her husband had died of D.T. I added that I'd four witnesses who were prepared to testify in court.

That frightened her. She started to say that she'd been 'under a misapprehension', but I cut her short. I said there'd been no misapprehension whatever, that I'd told her exactly what had happened and that her story had been a deliberate and malicious lie. At this she collapsed. I would be going too far to say that she apologized, but she came within sight of doing so; and when I said I hoped she would not stop Oliver coming to Orchards in the future, she agreed to put me 'in bounds' again. In fact, we parted almost amicably.

Now more Bose; I find him irresistible. At Faridpore, near Calcutta, there was a celebrated leaning date-palm which bowed its head at the time of evening prayer.

No doubt about it: Bose gives two photographs. The usual story: pilgrimages to the 'praying' palm, alleged miraculous cures, and speculators making fortunes by buying up land. Bose decided to investigate.

The locals weren't co-operative—they didn't like the idea of a rational explanation which would ruin trade—and he had a good deal of difficulty in getting permission to attach recording instruments to the tree. He found that the palm actually moved all the time, and that the movements coincided with changes of temperature. When it was hottest (about 3.15 p.m.), it bowed its lowest. This was about an hour earlier than evening prayer; 'but people who are out to impute miracles would not be disturbed in their faith by such a slight discrepancy'.

A year later Bose was lecturing on the subject in Calcutta when a telegram arrived from Faridpore to say the palm had died. Lord Ronaldshay, the Governor of Bengal, who was in the chair, read it out: 'The palm-tree is dead and its movements have ceased.' The local Press suggested that the palm had committed suicide to avoid the exposure of its fraud.

Bose soon found himself a sorting-house for vegetable wonders of this kind. There was a weeping Mango in Calcutta, and a Praying Willow (vouched for by a Church of England clergyman) near Liverpool. There were coconut trees in South Africa which curtseyed at sunset, presumably to let their owners pick the fruit. Bose came to the conclusion that all inclined trees moved, but that the movement wasn't noticed unless the inclination was so great that the ground became a point of reference by which to check it.

Though I'm miles from the nearest cathedral, my chrysanthemums have been invaded by the Bishop Bug (*Lygus pratensis*); I'm following Wilson's advice and shaking 'immature and mature bugs on dull days into an open inverted umbrella'.

September 24th

I'm *delighted* to hear that you are coming home next week, and I shall much look forward to seeing you here. I can see no reason why you shouldn't pay me that visit that was fixed for last autumn. Anyhow I shall come over to Kingsmead as soon as I possibly can.

When you read what follows, you'll really begin to believe that alcohol is fated to play a disastrous role in my life: first Oliver, and now Susanna. In short, I've narrowly escaped committing womanslaughter. This is what happened:

I'd told Susanna, who'd been working in the garden after tea, to help herself to a drink; she poured herself out a large gin and French, took a sip and said, 'This tastes *very* peculiar'. No doubt it did: she was drinking gin and Growquick!

It was partly my fault, partly Mrs. Benham's. I'd used an old vermouth bottle, but I *had* put a large POISON label on it; Mrs. Benham—tidy soul!—had noticed the bottle in the loggia and brought it in and put it on the drinks tray. Susanna suddenly caught sight of the label (actually I'd no idea whether the stuff was poisonous or not) and immediately decided that she was dying—if not actually dead; she became completely hysterical. I gave her a strong emetic and rang up Dr. Brown, who came rushing round with a stomach-pump. It was, as you may imagine, all very unpleasant. It was probably Susanna's favourite recipe—nine-tenths gin and one-tenth vermouth—that saved her; which goes to show the wisdom of taking one's drinks strong. But supposing I'd put the Growquick into a *gin* bottle . . .

Last week in Oxford I bought at Blackwell's, for a sum so small that I'd hate Sir Basil to know, a sixteenth-century manuscript of Sadi's *Gulistan*, or 'Rose Garden' —the most popular of all Persian books (I shall leave it to you in my will). The miniatures in it, though damaged, are lovely: one has a *chenar* (oriental plane) that would have pleased Xerxes, and in another a youth plucks a spray of almond blossom from a tree that's enchantingly patterned against a gold sky. At the same time I bought Eastwick's translation, first published in 1852.

The *Gulistan* is a collection of moral tales written by Sadi in Shiraz in the thirteenth century. In his preface he tells how, 'it being the season of spring, when the asperity of winter was mitigated and the time of the roses' rich display had arrived', he decided to write the book; I've copied out a bit of it for you because, in spite of its artificiality, I liked it so much:

> One night it happened that I was walking at a late hour in a flower garden with one of my friends. The spot was blithe and pleasing, and the trees intertwined there charmingly. You would have said that fragments of enamel were sprinkled on the ground, and that the necklace of the Pleiades was suspended from the vines that grew there. . . . In the morning, when the inclination to return prevailed over our wish to stay, I saw that he had gathered his lap full of roses, fragrant herbs, hyacinths and sweet basil, with which he was setting out for the city.
>
> I said, 'To the rose of the garden there is, as you know, no continuance. . . . The sages have said that we should not fix our affections on that which has no endurance. . . . For the recreation of the beholders and the gratification of those who are present, I am able to compose a book, THE GARDEN OF ROSES, whose leaves the rude hand of the blast of autumn cannot affect, and the blitheness of whose spring the

revolution of time cannot change into the disorder of the waning year. . . .'

Don't you think there's an almost Elizabethan freshness in this? Some time I'll send you an English piece about daffodils which seems to me to have the same sort of flavour.

Positively the last instalment of Bose, I promise you; but he so fascinates me that I can't resist. Bose's great trouble when he came to study the growth of plants, was that they grow so slowly. Even the snail travels 2,000 times as fast as the tip of a quick-growing plant-shoot. So he constructed what he called the High Magnification Crescograph. It worked by levers, magnified the rate of growth 10,000 times and recorded it on a smoked glass plate. This made the plant-shoot appear to grow six inches in a minute, and the snail to move at the rate of an express train.

Most people would have been satisfied with this, but Bose wasn't. Next came the Balanced Crescograph, and finally the Magnetic Crescograph. This amazing machine used mirrors to magnify growth-movement up to a hundred million times. The plant-shoots now seemed to move with the speed of a galloping horse, and the snail with that of an astronaut!

Bose made a lot of interesting discoveries with his Crescographs. He found that the growth of a shoot was pulsatory—'not steady, but like the wavelets of a rising tide'. He showed that it was affected by wireless waves, and by a single flash of (artificial) lightning. Having

T

for a brief spell been a schoolmaster, I was amused to learn that he had demonstrated that rough handling harmed a vigorous plant but stimulated a backward one. And finally he trained a plant to turn on the electric light when it grew dark, and turn it off when it became light again. It reacted even to 'a passing fog. This device', he wrote, 'may prove useful during winter in London'.

Universities all over the world begged Bose to come and lecture to them, and he was in full swing when the First World War broke out. He died in the 1920s, but his work is carried on by the Bose Institute in Calcutta.

Don't you agree that he must have been a glorious man?

Helen Parker has been to a sherry party at the Stringers', to which I couldn't go. 'What on *earth* has happened to Mrs. P.?' she said to me. 'I overheard her telling Colonel Stringer that you'd been such a help to Oliver over his music. I could hardly believe my ears. I suppose she's now decided that Susanna is public enemy number one.' I must admit that she's made very handsome amends. There's not much doubt that she was thoroughly *frightened*, and I expect that Susanna's attack has also helped to make her realize that she isn't much loved by a good many of the local inhabitants.

P.S. I see in Murray's *Handbook for Travellers in Asia Minor* (1895 ed.) that 'Mush has the reputation of being the filthiest town in Turkey. . . . Some of the women wear nose-rings.' How I'd love to see Susanna wearing hers!

September 28th

I picked up the other day in Dorking, for half-a-crown the pair, two little books that have entertained me.

One is *Flowers and Gardens*, by Forbes Watson, published post-humously in 1872. Watson was a young Nottingham surgeon who died at the age of 29. During his last long agonizing illness he took comfort in recalling the flowers he loved, and I find that his views are almost exactly the same as mine. For example, after describing a visit to a very stiff and formal tulip show he mentions that, on his way out, he came upon a couple of 'altogether untrained' tulips growing in an unweeded bed; 'I would sooner,' he wrote, 'have had those two neglected flowers than all the exhibition.' How often, staggering away half-dazed and half-blinded from the marquees at Chelsea, have I too been revived by the sight of a common dandelion that the gardeners have overlooked. Here are a few bits from Watson's book:

> My chief accusation is, that gardeners are teaching us to think too little about the plants individually, and to look at them chiefly as an assemblage of beautiful colours.

> None can have a healthy love for flowers unless he loves the wild ones.

> Nine people have an eye for colour to one who thinks about form.

> In spring I like to have two or three bright scarlet Anemones (*hortensis*), with two or three spikes of Grape Hyacinth (*racemosum*), two Jonquils, two pieces of white Ranunculus, two brown Fritillaries (*Pyrenaica*) and two white ones, and a single stem of the large pink Saxifrage, and all these intermixed and put together loosely in a small vase, so as to look as if they were growing in a meadow, but growing unusually close.

> Think of gardeners stigmatizing, as I am told is the case, the Lilac and Laburnum as plebeian! To what pitch of degradation must that man's taste have sunk who could reject and despise so elegant a tree as the Laburnum!

> Common people will generally prefer the highly-cultivated flower to the simple one, just for that one

quality of bigness and plumpness. In the same way, most vulgar people admire great red-faced women, and judge of the beauty of prize pigs and oxen by their size.

But what are we the better for Anemones six inches across?

Never fear to admire old-fashioned flowers because they are spoken of with contempt.

Watson was, of course, an ardent Ruskinian; but his book was written some years before Ruskin began *Proserpina* or William Robinson *The Wild Garden*, and he must have been something of a pioneer.

The other book is called *The Language of Flowers*: no author, no date; but it was given 'to Millie from Mr. and Mrs. Watts, wishing her many happy returns of the day', on June 20th, 1887. By means of a carefully composed bouquet and two copies of the book, lovers could communicate with one another secretly. For example, here is a bunch—though admittedly one that it might not be easy to assemble:

A truffle	You surprise me.
A sprig of larch	How dare you!
Monarda amplexicaulis	Your whims are unbearable.
A spray of furze	I am very angry with you.
Purple columbine	I think you silly
Dahlia	(and) very feeble.
Ziphion spinosum	Be prudent.
Dogsbane	Your friend is deceitful,

Queen's rocket	(and) you are the queen of coquettes.
Virginia spiderwort	Your happiness won't last.
Dark geranium	I am very miserable;
A filbert	do make up our quarrel.
Pimpernel	Will you grant me an interview?
Stephanotis	Will you accompany me to the East?
Thrift	You are a good little housewife.
Calceolaria	I offer you my fortune; or, I offer you pecuniary aid.
Virginia creeper	I cling to you both in sunshine and shade.
Mouse-eared scorpion-grass	Do not forget me.

Don't you think it's *just* the thing for Susanna?

Ever your very affectionate godfather

Wilfrid Sharp

OCTOBER

October 2nd

My dearest Flora,

I've just been 'looking in' on 'the strange adventures of Yogi Bear, Snagglepuss and Yakky Doodle Duck' on I.T.V.; when one lives alone, one sometimes does the oddest things. How horrified your dear mother, so vehement on the subject of television (without, I gather, having ever actually seen it), would be if she knew! I had begun by listening to a 'Beethoven —Bouton-Moulez sonata recital'—you know how the Third Programme adores to bring together the works of the distinguished dead and the lunatic living —but I'd turned Bouton-Moulez off after the tenth bar.

Alas, I can't manage Monday afternoon, although I shall in fact be in London; I have a dreary committee meeting which I just can't cut. Get your mother to drive you to the *side* entrance of the Victoria and Albert (in Exhibition Road); it's nearer to the Print Room.

I'm so glad you are going to look at some flower drawings. I wish more people realized that these lovely things are there and to be seen for the asking. People are so shy of entering print rooms, and of 'giving trouble'; but this is a service that we all pay for. There's such a surfeit of flower prints and of coloured reproductions of prints and drawings nowadays, and most people have never even seen a good original.

I suggest that, for a start, you look at the work of three artists: Le Moyne de Morgues, Johann Walther and Georg Ehret—representing the sixteenth, seventeenth and eighteenth centuries respectively.

Le Moyne was a Huguenot who came over here after St. Bartholomew and was taken up by the Sidneys. The V. & A. has a dismembered album of his charming, unpretentious little drawings, and the British Museum has just bought a more showy one. Le Moyne's is amateur work in the true sense of the word—a labour of love. Lord Pheen would like it.

Walther was employed by Count Johann of Nassau to paint the flowers in his garden near Frankfurt. His work is entirely different from Le Moyne's. Le Moyne painted humble flowers (many of them wild flowers) humbly; Walther's patron wanted his more sensational flowers made to look as sensational as possible. So these are decorative paintings—so decorative, indeed, that I'm very surprised that they haven't yet caught the eye of a publisher or table-mat manufacturer.

You could call Ehret—a German who spent the best years of his life in England—the Handel of flower painters. His paintings, like Handel's music, are triumphant, magnificent. But you'll notice that Ehret was a trained botanist who didn't allow art to swamp science. Of all flower painters he was perhaps the most successful in reconciling this difficult pair. I shall be very interested to hear which of my three you like best. I don't suppose you'll be surprised that my own choice is Le Moyne.

All well here—except that Mrs. Benham has suddenly taken to adding fronds of asparagus to every bunch of flowers I arrange. It's maddening: I make three roses look nice in a tumbler, go off for five minutes to the Post Office, and return to find three bits of asparagus ruining everything. She says she read in a woman's paper that it was 'the fashion'. However, she now shows signs of a new craze which may take her mind off asparagus: Britain's Independent Nuclear 'Detergent'.

Oh, and the moles: we are overrun by them! I do wish they hadn't got those 'highly fossorial fore feet': they make such mountains out of their mole-hills. G. F. Wilson suggests, in the R.H.S. Dictionary, various ways of dealing with the mole—'a timid animal, strong in its digging powers, acute of hearing, voracious in appetite'. Ovenden and I have tried a few of the less unattractive of these; but neither of us can face 'dipping large earthworms in strychnine', which is Wilson's strongest recommendation.

I've fallen in love with a little late-flowering, lilac-coloured pink which came originally, I believe, from cuttings of a plant brought back by Robert Gathorne-Hardy from Greece; I've no idea what it's called. I now know all its little ways: the varying forms of the petals, which are sometimes fringed and sometimes merely serrated; its determined sprawling habit which brings it into open conflict with the lawn-mower; the exquisite rhythms of its petals and stamens. But above all I love it for flowering—rather shyly, I admit—in October, and for having such a delicious smell. I must try to propagate it for you.

This will amuse you. The other day Delia found a very scruffy-looking man at the back door, who said, almost reproachfully, 'Don't you recognize me, ma'am? I'm your burglar'! Delia immediately asked him in, fed him, showed him round her best silver and gave him a pound. It's not reported whether or not she called him 'Darling'.

The carbohydrates and albuminous materials are emigrating from the leaves, and anthocyanins and anthoxanthones are developing: in other words, the autumn tints are beginning. All other news when we meet on Wednesday.

October 9th

I needn't tell you what a joy it was seeing you and finding you in such splendid form. I shall look forward to having you here in a fortnight's time, after which I suppose we shall rarely find you south of the Border.

Mrs. Puttenham asked me to what proved to be a tête-à-tête lunch on Sunday, and I felt I ought to bury the hatchet and accept. She was extremely nervous, and she certainly laid herself out to be as amiable as possible. She asked me what I would like to drink, and I could see her hand tremble as she poured out the gin. At lunch she thanked me for 'taking an interest' in Oliver (who was, of course, 'so highly strung'), and asked my advice about his future. Was it enough for him to have five mornings a week coaching from the Rector? He was nearly sixteen now, and so *young* for his age. Should she send him to Paris to learn French?

The idea of Oliver loose in Paris didn't commend itself to me. I said that since he was no good at his books, but seemed genuinely keen on gardening, wouldn't it be better to send him to an agricultural college or something of that kind? And meanwhile, why shouldn't he learn as much as he could from Chandler?

She winced when Chandler's name was mentioned; but she agreed that it might be a good idea. She's going to enquire about a possible college, and meanwhile Oliver will help Chandler in the greenhouses and come to me also. So I'm very glad I took action. There's a lot of good in Oliver (and even in Mrs. Puttenham?) if it can be properly directed. The first thing to do is to get him away from his mother, but to somewhere where he is reasonably under supervision.

What a charming nation we're becoming! Last Wednesday three Teddy boys went to the village shop and asked Mr. Peters if he could let them have glasses of water as they were thirsty. When Peters turned to fetch them some, they hit him over the back of the head with a piece of lead piping and left him unconscious. They then robbed the till, smashed up the shop, and on the way out kicked (out of sheer malice) the gnome and the gnomery to pieces. Peters is not on the danger list but he's feeling pretty sorry for himself. As soon as I heard I went to see if I could be of any help, only to find that Mrs. Puttenham—repeat, Mrs. Puttenham!— had everything in hand and had said that she herself would cover any loss or expense not covered by insurance. It just shows how one can get people wrong: I would have been prepared to wager any money that Mrs. P. would have 'passed by on the other side'. I now believe the story Helen told me. I've also heard from Usher that she gave quite a large sum to the church tower appeal and wished the gift to be anonymous. I couldn't resist going to tell Delia, who was as astonished as I was; I added how amiable Mrs. P. had been when I lunched with her. Delia said, 'Darling! I really believe you're *in love* with that awful woman!' The remark was so absurd that I didn't bother to answer.

I've just purchased, for three shillings, something

which, 'if left undisturbed in a good location, will bring its message of joy' to my garden for several years: in other words, a 'multiflora' hyacinth. So much happiness seems cheap at the price. The carton containing the bulb is covered with uplift in various languages. The French, for example, are promised 'une multitude de fleurs odorifiques', and the Germans much the same— but for neither is there a message of joy. I would love to know what the Finns can hope for, but I can't begin to guess the meaning of words like 'kukkaruukkuihin'.

Goodnight, my dearest Multiflora; it's past midnight and I can't keep my eyes open another second—not even to write to *you*!

October 16th

Here are my daffodils for you. They come from a
letter written in 1610 by Ralph Cunnynghame to his
cousin, Sir Robert Stapleton, who was in London. I
wonder whether Wordsworth knew it; it's hard to
believe that he didn't. I must investigate:

> Yestermorn I was abroad while the dewe still laye
> upon the grasse, for it was sweete and bright. I
> knowe not what it is that bringeth at such tymes of
> spring a fullness of joye to the heart, but so it is, and
> certes was with me especiallie on this sweet daye, for
> alle thinges were budding tenderlie, and the whole
> worlde seemed full of pure delighte. . . .

He walked through meadows 'carpeted with the
daintie beauties of manie flowers', the song of the lark
falling 'like a sweet shower of praise from the golden
skye', till his 'hearte did fairly ake with keen bliss-
fullnesse':

> And soe at last I came to a certaine spott I wotted of
> where alle around the bankes of a tiny lakelet stood a
> whole hoste of Daffodillies growne talle and statelie
> and fayre; neither coulde there haue been lesse than
> thousandes of them, so that the whole earthe co-
> adjacent seemed strewn thick with bright yellow
> flakes of golde; and whenever a smalle wynde came
> they bowed in greate rowes lyke a sea of golden
> starrs. I know not why it was, Amadis, but certes my
> hearte was so flooded with a bliss and strong love

longinge that big teares of tender joye did fill mine
eyes, and soe I lay me downe upon a greene banke of
Grasse and sweete herbes, and gazed at those fayre
blossoms with gentle joyance. . . .

You'll hardly need to be told that at that very instant
the sweetest conceivable mayde popped out of ye
undergrowth. . . . I know it's absurd: just pastoral
silliness; but all the same I enjoy it—in very small
doses.

Since I last wrote to you I've been doing something
highly improbable: writing the first of a series of six
articles on 'Teeth: past, present and future' for a perfectly serious dental quarterly (you shall see them in
due course). The paper has a new Editor who came to
the conclusion (rightly, I'm sure) that his paper was
unreadable. So he decided that people who knew about
teeth couldn't write, and people who could write
didn't know about teeth. And having read some articles
by myself that had amused him (those ones in *Punch*),
he asked me if I'd be willing to do something light-
hearted for him if he provided me with the material and
vetted the result. I agreed. You know, it's not quite so
silly as it sounds. I'm constantly reading botanical
books that have been ruined by their authors' total
ignorance of anything outside botany. I've often
thought when reading Ruskin, 'Si Ruskin savait, si les
botanistes pouvaient.'

So I set to work. Do you know, if I *do* have any
quality that is not so very common, I believe it's the

capacity to become enormously interested—*for a time*—in almost any odd thing that comes my way. I've been reading Urbain Hémard's *Researches upon the Anatomy of Teeth* (1582) as eagerly as if it were a detective story, and I can hardly put down the back numbers of the 'American Journal of Dental Science' sent me by my Editor. I had a great day at the Natural History Museum among the mammoth tusks. How exciting everything is when you start examining it! I'm really quite looking forward to my next visit to the dentist.

I'm sorry to say that the Admiral is in what he calls 'a fwightfully wetched state'. He's been in bed for a month and there's something seriously wrong with his heart. He'd been warned more than once to go slow with his tree-felling, but he wouldn't listen. I take him flowers and tried to lend him books; but he'll only read 'yarns' about the sea and biographies of Admirals, so I've had to get them for him from the Dorking Public Library.

He's supposed to be 'on the water-wagon', as he calls it, but yesterday he insisted upon opening a bottle of champagne so that we could drink to his recovery. 'Here's to more tree-felling,' I said. 'Only in future they must be *small* trees.' But he knows how things are: 'I'll never fell another twee,' he said sadly. And I'm pretty sure he never will; there's every chance that he'll recover if he behaves sensibly, and I think he's been healthily scared this time. As I was leaving he asked me if I could guess who had sent him the champagne. I presumed it had come from Delia, who is responsible for almost every kind act done locally; but I said half jokingly, 'No doubt the Lady of the Manor being munificent.' And do you know—it *was*!

I'll be with you today week at about 11 o'clock, then we can get back here in good time for lunch. Delia is coming, and I've actually managed to capture Lord Pheen too. It should make a nice *partie carrée*.

I'm simply longing to show you the garden. I've now, of course, seen a full year round and watched order gradually emerge out of chaos; but *you* haven't seen it since I got to work on it, and I believe you'll be surprised. My only regret is that I didn't have it photographed last autumn; I might have done an article for Roy Hay.

I think the terrace is the first thing that will strike you. The petunias in the big tubs are getting straggly now; but they're still a mass of flower, and only yesterday I counted fifty-two morning glories. Then that long strip of what appeared to be a meadow punctuated by tops of urns and heads of nymphs—the strip leading from the terrace down to the wild garden and stream— is now a stone-paved walk with statuary and herbaceous borders on either side. (I know that herbaceous borders are out of fashion, but none the less I like them.) The plantation of 'old' roses beyond the lawn is more or less flowerless at the moment, but you'll be able to imagine what it was like in June and, I hope, see it next June in still greater glory. As for the lawn itself—well, at all events it's better, though your dear mother still refers to it as 'elephant grass'.

The colchicums I put in have been good but they're

U

almost over. However, the autumn crocuses (I planted a thousand) are just at their best—a great sheet of various lavenders and white. All that beauty, year after year, for an initial outlay of only eight or nine pounds! Next year, if I can afford it, I'll plant a thousand more: one can't have too many. The rest of the wild garden is still rather wilder in parts than it should be, and the stream is only partly cleared; I'm getting down to them now.

But why go on? Next week—bless you!—you shall see it all for yourself.

October 28th

No—all the thanks are due to *you*. It was a memorable visit for me, and next summer I hope you'll come again and bring Angus with you.

There *is* one piece of local news: Usher is engaged to Helen Parker! I admit that I was astonished when I heard it. I knew that Helen had yearned for years, and I realized that Usher was dreading the prospect of living alone; and they are both keen gardeners. But I hadn't quite expected that particular solution of their problems. I dare say it will work out reasonably well, though I must confess that the thought of Helen at breakfast, lunch, tea and dinner—I can't imagine it will involve more than that—would give *me* pause. . . .

Susanna is bursting with excitement over an 'Italian' composer whom she's just discovered—'Poorchéll', she called him. It was quite a time before I tumbled to it that she meant Purcell.

And now we shan't meet again until the DAY!

Forgive this scrawl; I'm in a hurry.

October 30th

Yes, of course I'll be delighted and proud to propose your health at the wedding. I *won't* be facetious, and I *won't* rake up embarrassing stories of your childhood! In fact, to be quite honest I'd rather cut the speech and just wish you both what we all wish you—many years of happiness. I'm very glad we aren't to wear those silly clothes; I was afraid your mother might insist.

It's nice of you to say that you've enjoyed my rambling letters, though I can hardly believe that they speeded up your convalescence. You'll soon have a full-time job running a house and looking after a husband, so in future I'll be brief. Perhaps I shall find another bedridden botanist who would like to be at the receiving end of my effusions!

Your mother has asked me to do the flowers for the house; I gather that the church flowers have been put in the hands of the professionals. This at least I'll promise you—that there won't be any wet silver paint around! But I suppose it will have to be chiefly chrysanthemums again; now if only you'd got married in June....!

Ever your very affectionate godfather

Wilfrid Sharp

NOVEMBER

November 6th

My dearest Flora,

Last night I dined with Delia—just the two of us—and we talked until after midnight. Though we've known each other for a year now, this was the first time that we'd ever discussed serious matters. She told me about her parents and her childhood in Scotland, her schooldays, her time at Cambridge, her marriage, and the anxious war years when Humphrey was serving abroad; I think that a large part of her charm lies in the fact that she combines a masculine mind with feminine failings. I too spoke of past happinesses and unhappinesses—things I've talked of with no one since Betty died.

I'd come on foot—my car is in dock—and Delia wanted to drive me home. But I felt that I needed cool air and to walk. The moon was almost full, a little veiled by thin cloud, and the mist waist-high over the water-meadows. The air was full of dank autumn smells —of fallen leaves and water-mint and farmyards; and the silence seemed to sing. Then suddenly I saw in the meadows something so ridiculous that I burst out laughing: *a horse without any legs*! Its body was sailing on the waves of a white sea, like a child's rubber toy at the seaside. For a moment I thought I'd go back and fetch Delia; it was just her sort of joke. But it was really too late.

I walked into the field to take a closer look; and then, on a mad impulse, I decided to attempt the short cut across the meadows. Even by daylight it's a tricky path, and I soon realized that I'd lost it. Meanwhile the mist was rising steadily. Twice I fell, covering myself with mud. I tried to get my bearings from the moon, but I miscalculated and found myself almost in the stream. Half an hour must have passed before I eventually met the horse again—now just a head!—and so finally found the gate.

Very tired and very wet, yet curiously elated, I walked back along the road to the village, meditating on Life, and why we were here at all, and where—if anywhere—we might be going. As I reached the gates of the Manor the church clock struck one and immediately, not a hundred yards away from me, there was a loud bang: a rocket soared up into the sky and burst into splintering stars. I could see a smouldering bonfire near the spot where it had risen from; no doubt it was a rocket overlooked by the Puttenhams in their Guy Fawkes celebrations, and the bonfire had set it off.

Lights appeared in various windows in the village

street, and heads popped out; it was just like that bit
near the end of the second Act of *Die Meistersinger*!
Very aware that I must present a pretty bedraggled and
peculiar appearance, I took refuge in some bushes just
inside the Manor gates, intending to stay hidden until
the heads had popped in again. And there, crouching
guiltily, covered from head to foot in mud, I suddenly
found myself a ludicrous and unwilling display of *son et
lumière* in the blinding floodlight of the village policeman's torch! I don't think he believed a single word of
my *son*, and for a moment I thought he was going to
take me into custody.

Mrs. Benham dried and brushed and pressed my
clothes and asked no questions; no doubt she imagined
I'd had a night 'on the tiles', and it seemed too difficult
to explain what had really happened. But the policeman is a notorious gossip, and my reputation in Dewbury is now ruined for ever. Why, only a moment ago
Delia rang up and said, 'Darling, are you all right?'

'Of course I'm all right,' I said. 'Why shouldn't I
be?'

'I mean, Darling, you *did* get home all right last
night?'

'Of course I did. It was a *lovely* evening. What are
you driving at?'

'O Darling, I'm *so* relieved. It's just that my gardener
says that you were found dead drunk in a ditch at
4 o'clock this morning. Isn't it quite fantastic what lies
gardeners tell? It's worse than Ovenden and his mandrake!'

'Far worse,' I said. 'Darling, it *was* a lovely evening, and THANK YOU! But on the way home I *did* see a horse without any legs.'

Ever your very affectionate godfather

Wilfrid Sharp